Grade 2

Scott Foresman

Phonics and Spelling Practice Book

SAVVAS
LEARNING COMPANY

ISBN-13: 978-0-328-14647-5
ISBN-10: 0-328-14647-1
37 20

Contents

Unit 3 Creative Ideas

Unit 4 Our Changing World

Unit 5 Responsibility

Unit 6 Traditions

Steps for Spelling New Words

Here is a plan to use when you study your spelling words.

Step 1
Look at the word. **Say** it and listen to the sounds.

Step 2
Spell the word aloud.

Step 3
Think about the spelling. Is there anything special to remember?

Step 4
Picture the word with your eyes shut.

Step 5
Look at the word and **write** it.

Step 6
Cover the word. Picture it and **write** it again. **Check** its spelling. Did you get it right?

Spelling Practice Book

There are 6 steps to remember. Use this plan a few times. You will see how it can help you.

 Joe wants to learn the new spelling word *mice*.
In Step 1, he looks at the word, says it, and listens to all the sounds.

 In Step 2, he spells the word aloud.

 In Step 3, he thinks about how the word is spelled.

 In Step 4, Joe sees the word with his eyes shut.

 In Step 5, Joe looks at the word and he writes it on paper at the same time.

 Finally, in Step 6, Joe covers the word. He pictures what it looks like. Then he writes it again. He checks to see if it is correct.

Rhyming Helpers

If you can match a new list word to a word you know with the same spelling at the end, you will have two words that rhyme. Then the old word can be a helper for the new word. These words are Rhyming Helpers.

Hop is the rhyming helper for *chop*. *Chop* and *hop* rhyme and they have the same ending.

Gave is the rhyming helper for *brave*. They rhyme and have the same ending.

Boat is Ken's rhyming helper for float. Watch out! Some words rhyme but have different spellings. The word *note* sounds like *boat*, but the rhyming sound is spelled in a different way. *Boat* ends in **o-a-t**, *note* ends in **o-t-e**. *Note* is NOT a rhyming helper for *boat*. Here is more practice on Rhyming Helpers.

One of your new spelling words is *clown*.
You already know how to spell *down*.
Down is the rhyming helper for *clown*.

Rhyming Helper   **New spelling word**
down   **clown**

Both words have the same ending. Now you can remember
how the ending of *clown* is spelled. It is just like *down*!

Sometimes, thinking about the rhyming words in a
short sentence will help you remember how they
work together.

The **clown** fell **down**.

Remember, some words rhyme but they have different
spellings. Those are NOT rhyming helpers.

The word *noun* sounds like *clown*, but the rhyming sound
is spelled in a different way. *Noun* is not a rhyming helper.

down   clown   ~~noun~~

Problem Parts

Everybody has words that are hard to spell. Sometimes the problem is with a few letters. This is a good time to use the **Problem Parts** strategy.

One of the words you will learn is *breeze*.

The word *breeze* has an e sound, but how do you spell it? That is tricky! Here are steps to follow to use the Problem Parts strategy.

Step 1
Ask yourself which part of the word is giving you a problem.

Step 2
Write the word and underline the problem part.

Step 3
Picture the word. Focus on what the problem part looks like. Sometimes you might want to picture the problem part in large letters to help.

Now picture your word. See the hard part before you try to spell it.

Dividing Long Words

Long words can be very hard to learn to spell. The Dividing Long Words strategy can help you spell these words.

Use syllables to make long words easier to study.

Step 1

Say the word slowly. Listen for the syllables.

Step 2

Write the word and draw lines between the syllables.

Step 3

Study the word one syllable at a time.

Here are three more long words. They have been divided into parts to show you how the Dividing Long Words strategy works.

disappear = dis | ap | pear   basketball = bas | ket | ball

happiness = hap | pi | ness

Long words are easier to spell when you break them into smaller parts.

Frequently Misspelled Words!

The words below are words that are misspelled the most by students your age. Pay special attention to these frequently misspelled words as you read, write, and spell.

because	once	thought	swimming
too	again	want	where
they	didn't	two	don't
when	scared	about	family
there	that's	every	into
went	house	whole	them
their	Halloween	before	tried
Christmas	with	could	was
people	very	like	beautiful
favorite	baseball	started	brother
friends	heard	to	different
were	then	some	found
said	what	it's	have
our	everybody	took	knew
a lot	I	special	nice
would	and	they're	one
upon	another	through	there's
know	little	caught	watch
friend	first	really	
outside	night	other	
Easter	sometimes	presents	

Spelling Practice Book

Short Vowels CVC, CVCC, CCVC

Generalization Short vowels are often spelled **a**: s<u>a</u>d, **e**: d<u>e</u>sk, **i**: r<u>i</u>b, **o**: j<u>o</u>b, **u**: dr<u>u</u>m.

Sort the list words by the short vowel.

a

1. _____

2. _____

3. _____

e

4. _____

5. _____

11. _____

Challenge Words

e

13. _____

15. _____

o

6. _____

7. _____

8. _____

u

9. _____

10. _____

i

12. _____

o

14. _____

Spelling Words

1. drum
2. rock
3. list
4. desk
5. job
6. sad
7. chop
8. sack
9. tag
10. rib
11. mess
12. dust

Challenge Words

13. pocket
14. lettuce
15. engine

Home Activity Your child is learning to spell words with short vowels and these consonant/vowel patterns: CVC, CVCC, CCVC. To practice at home, have your child look at the word, pronounce it, and then write it.

Short Vowels CVC, CVCC, CCVC

Write a list word to finish the rhyme.

Spelling Words	
drum	chop
rock	sack
list	tag
desk	rib
job	mess
sad	dust

1. gum on a
_____
- - - - - - - - - - - - - - -
_____

2. Zack in a
_____
- - - - - - - - - - - - - - -
_____

3. bag with a
_____
- - - - - - - - - - - - - - -
_____

4. lock on a
_____
- - - - - - - - - - - - - - -
_____

5. Tess is a
_____
- - - - - - - - - - - - - - -
_____

6. fist with a
_____
- - - - - - - - - - - - - - -
_____

Write a list word to finish the sentence.

dust
job
sad
chop
rib
desk

_____
- - - - - - - - - - - - - - -
7. Tom's _____ was to set the table.

_____
- - - - - - - - - - - - - - - - -
8. My teacher sits at a _____ .

_____
- - - - - - - - - - - - - - -
9. Will you _____ this apple?

_____
- - - - - - - - - - - - - - - -
10. Get a rag and _____ the bench.

_____
- - - - - - - - - - - - - - -
11. Sara was _____ when her dog got lost.

_____
- - - - - - - - - - - - - - -
12. Andy fell and hurt his _____ .

Home Activity Your child wrote words with short vowels and these consonant/vowel patterns: CVC, CVCC, CCVC. Give clues about a word. Say, for example, "You play it in a band. It has a short *u*." Have your child guess and spell the word (drum).

Spelling Practice Book

Short Vowels CVC, CVCC, CCVC

Read the report Jenny wrote. Circle two spelling mistakes. Write the words correctly. Then write Jenny's last sentence correctly.

> The artist took som clay out of a sak. It looked like a rock. He put it on the desk. He made it into a bird. The desk was a mess. The bird very pretty.

Spelling Words

drum	chop
rock	sack
list	tag
desk	rib
job	mess
sad	dust

_____ _____

1. _____ 2. _____

3. _____

Frequently Misspelled Words

with

have

them

some

Circle the word that is spelled correctly. **Write** it.

_____

4. dus   dust   _____

5. drum   drun   _____

6. chopp   chop   _____

7. job   jub   _____

8. list   lis   _____

Home Activity Your child has identified and corrected misspelled words with short vowels and these consonant/vowel patterns: CVC, CVCC, CCVC. Have your child spell one of the words and then change a vowel to make another word. For example, the word *rib* could become *rob* or *rub*.

Spelling Practice Book

Unit 1 Week 1 **Day 3** **3**

Short Vowels CVC, CVCC, CCVC

Circle the list words in the puzzle. Some words go across. Some go down. **Write** each word.

m	r	s	d	t	a	g
e	i	g	s	k	r	b
s	b	o	c	h	o	p
s	s	a	d	s	u	j
d	u	s	t	m	d	o
e	l	i	s	t	o	b

Spelling Words

drum	chop
rock	sack
list	tag
desk	rib
job	mess
sad	dust

chop
list
sad
tag
mess
dust
job
rib

1. _____

2. _____

3. _____

4. _____

5. _____

6. _____

7. _____

8. _____

Home Activity Your child has been learning to spell words with short vowels and these consonant/vowel patterns: CVC, CVCC, CCVC. Suggest that your child illustrate some of the words on the list. Then have your child label the sketches.

Name _____

Long Vowels CVCe

Generalization Long vowels are often spelled **CVCe**: p<u>age</u>, f<u>ine</u>, n<u>ose</u>, t<u>une</u>.

Sort the list words by the long vowel spelling.

a

1. _____

2. _____

3. _____

4. _____

i

5. _____

6. _____

7. _____

Challenge Words

a

13. _____

u

15. _____

o

8. _____

9. _____

10. _____

u

11. _____

12. _____

i

14. _____

Spelling Words
1. tune
2. page
3. nose
4. space
5. size
6. fine
7. mice
8. late
9. cube
10. blaze
11. home
12. vote
Challenge Words
13. erase
14. spice
15. confuse

Home Activity Your child is learning to spell words with long vowel sounds (consonant-vowel-consonant-e.) To practice at home, have your child look at the word, say it, spell it and point to the long vowel sound.

Exploring Space
PRACTICE

Long Vowels CVCe

Spelling Words					
tune	page	nose	space	size	fine
mice	late	cube	blaze	home	vote

Write the list word that makes sense in both phrases.

hum a ____
____ the piano

1. _____

____ ten shirt
____ it to fit

2. _____

turn the ____
get a ____

3. _____

coming ____
a ____ news bulletin

4. _____

paid a ____
looks ____

5. _____

outer ____
____ for one more

6. _____

Write a list word that rhymes.

7. note _____

8. dome _____

9. maze _____

10. nice _____

11. rose _____

12. tube _____

Home Activity Your child spelled words that contain long vowels. Ask your child how all the spelling words are alike. (All have a long vowel sound and end with vowel-consonant-e.)

Spelling Practice Book

Long Vowels CVCe

Read the note Jeff wrote about his pets.
Circle three spelling mistakes. Write the words
correctly. Then write the last sentence and
add the missing subject.

> Some people do not lik mice, but I do.
> I have two pet mice at hom. One has a black
> knows. Think mice make fine pets.

Spelling Words	
tune	mice
page	late
nose	cube
space	blaze
size	home
fine	vote

1. _____ 2. _____ 3. _____

4. _____

Frequently Misspelled Words
nice
like
baseball

Circle the word that is spelled correctly. Write it.

5. blaze   _____
   blaiz

6. voat   _____
   vote

7. hom   _____
   home

8. page   _____
   paje

9. qube   _____
   cube

10. space   _____
    spase

Home Activity Your child has been learning to spell words with long vowels. Have your child write
a paragraph using some of the spelling words.

Long Vowels CVCe

Draw a path through the maze. Follow the words with long *a*. Write each word.

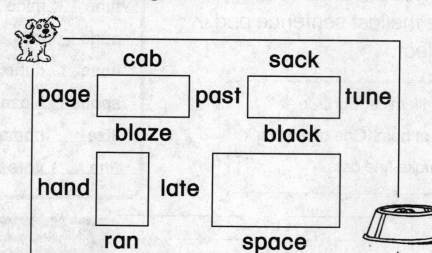

Spelling Words	
tune	mice
page	late
nose	cube
space	blaze
size	home
fine	vote

cab   sack

page [ ]   past [ ]   tune

blaze   black

hand [ ]   late [ ]

ran   space

1. _____   2. _____   3. _____   4. _____

Cross out the letters **p** and **a**. **Write** a list word by copying the letters that are left.

5. p h o a m e p _____

6. a a t u n p e p _____

7. a v a o t p e _____

8. a f p i p n e _____

9. s a p i z p e a _____

10. p a n o s a e p _____

Consonant Blends

Generalization Two or three consonants that are said together are called blends: <u>st</u>op, a<u>sk</u>, <u>str</u>ap.

Sort the list words by consonant blends.

sk

1. _____

2. _____

str

3. _____

4. _____

nd

5. _____

11. _____

st

6. _____

7. _____

8. _____

cl

9. _____

tw

10. _____

br

12. _____

Challenge Words

br

13. _____

sk

14. _____

str

15. _____

Spelling Words
1. stop
2. strap
3. nest
4. hand
5. brave
6. ask
7. clip
8. stream
9. mask
10. twin
11. breeze
12. state
Challenge Words
13. browse
14. straight
15. skeleton

Home Activity Your child is learning to spell words with consonant blends. To practice at home, help your child circle the letters that make up the consonant blend. Then ask your child to say each word.

Consonant Blends

Spelling Words					
stop	strap	nest	hand	brave	ask
clip	stream	mask	twin	breeze	state

Write a list word to complete each comparison.

1. Green means go. Red means _____ .

2. One of three is a triplet. One of two is a _____ .

3. A foot is on a leg. A _____ is on an arm.

4. A bee lives in a hive. A bird lives in a _____ .

5. A mitt goes on the hand. A _____ goes on the face.

6. Statements tell things. Questions _____ things.

Write the list word that means the same as the phrase.

7. cut off _____

8. full of courage _____

9. soft wind _____

10. leather strip _____

11. small river _____

12. part of U.S.A. _____

Home Activity Your child wrote words that contain consonant blends. Ask your child to circle each blend (st, str, nd, br, sk, cl, tw) and say its sound.

Spelling Practice Book

Name _____

Consonant Blends

Read the notice about the new ducklings. Find three spelling mistakes. Write the words correctly. Then write the first sentence with the missing end mark.

> Have you seen the ducklings? Take the path an stop at the sream You can see the nest in the grass near the twine pine trees.

Spelling Words

stop	clip
strap	stream
nest	mask
hand	twin
brave	breeze
ask	state

Frequently Misspelled Words

brother

and

went

I. _____ 2. _____ 3. _____

4. _____

Fill in the circle to show the correct spelling. **Write** the word.

_____

5. ○ brave   ○ brav   ○ bave

6. ○ stat   ○ state   ○ tate

7. ○ strap   ○ strape   ○ stap

8. ○ klip   ○ clipe   ○ clip

Home Activity Your child identified misspelled words with the consonant blends *st, str, nd, br, sk, cl,* and *tw*. Take turns thinking of other words with these blends.

Consonant Blends

Write the rhyming list word.

1. It begins like *twice*.
   It rhymes with *win*.

   _____

2. It begins like *stone*.
   It rhymes with *late*.

   _____

3. It begins like *brow*n.
   It rhymes with *freeze*.

   _____

4. It begins like *street*.
   It rhymes with *map*.

   _____

5. It begins like *straw*.
   It rhymes with *beam*.

   _____

Spelling Words	
stop	clip
strap	stream
nest	mask
hand	twin
brave	breeze
ask	state

Read the clues. **Write** the list words.
The words in the boxes will answer the riddle.

What has teeth but can never eat?

6. below the wrist

7. to trim

8. come to an end

9. a face covering

10. light wind

Home Activity Your child has been learning to spell words with consonant blends. Give your child a clue about a word and have him or her guess and spell the word.

Adding *-ed* and *-ing*

Generalization Some base words do not change when **-ed** or **-ing** is added: talk**ed**, lift**ing**. Others do change: drop**ped**, smil**ing**.

Sort the list words by type of ending.

Spelling Words

1. talked
2. talking
3. dropped
4. dropping
5. excited
6. exciting
7. lifted
8. lifting
9. hugged
10. hugging
11. smiled
12. smiling

Challenge Words

13. dragging
14. amazed
15. bouncing

-ed with no base word change

1. _____

2. _____

-ed with base word change

3. _____

4. _____

5. _____

6. _____

-ing with no base word change

7. _____

8. _____

-ing with base word change

9. _____

10. _____

11. _____

12. _____

Challenge Words

-ed with base word change

13. _____

-ing with base word change

14. _____

15. _____

Home Activity Your child is learning to spell words with *-ed* and *-ing*. To practice at home, have your child study the word, noting the ending, and then spell the word with eyes closed.

Adding *-ed* and *-ing*

Spelling Words					
talked	talking	dropped	dropping	excited	exciting
lifted	lifting	hugged	hugging	smiled	smiling

Write the list word to finish each sentence.

1. Kris is ____ her new kitten.

2. Are you very ____ about the game?

3. Dad ____ when he heard the joke.

4. You are ____ your plate.

5. She ____ the baby into the cart.

6. They ____ about the book.

1. _____

2. _____

3. _____

4. _____

5. _____

6. _____

Word Clues Write the list words that fit the clues.

It has an *-ed* ending. It has a double consonant.

7. _____   8. _____

It has an *-ing* ending. An e was dropped from the base word.

9. _____   10. _____

School + Home

Home Activity Your child wrote words that end with *-ed* or *-ing*. Say and spell a list word that has an *-ed* ending. Ask your child to spell the corresponding *-ing* word.

Name _____

Adding -ed and -ing

Read about Tara's problem. Circle three spelling mistakes. Write the words correctly. Cross out the incorrect end mark and rewrite the sentence.

> My friend talked to me about taking swiming lessons. I smileed and thought it would be exciteing, but now I am scared. Shall I quit.

Spelling Words	
talked	lifted
talking	lifting
dropped	hugged
dropping	hugging
excited	smiled
exciting	smiling

1. _____

2. _____

3. _____

4. _____

Frequently Misspelled Words

scared

swimming

Circle the word that is spelled correctly. **Write** it.

5. smiling
   smileing _____

6. droping
   dropping _____

7. huged
   hugged _____

8. exciting
   excitting _____

9. lifted
   liftted _____

10. dropped
    droped _____

Home Activity Your child identified misspelled words that end with -ed or -ing. Ask your child to explain how the base word changes when -ing is added to *smile* or *excite*. (The final *e* is dropped.)

Spelling Practice Book

Unit 1 Week 4 **Day 3** 15

Name _____

Adding -ed and -ing

Spelling Words					
talked	talking	dropped	dropping	excited	exciting
lifted	lifting	hugged	hugging	smiled	smiling

Write a list word that rhymes with the underlined word.

1. Mom <u>popped</u> in the door just as
   I ____ the plate.

2. We were just <u>walking</u> and ____.

3. Tom kept ____ while he was <u>filing</u>
   the papers.

Read the clue. **Write** the list word
that means the **opposite**.

Across
4. was speechless
8. boring

Down
5. dropping
6. picking up
7. frowned

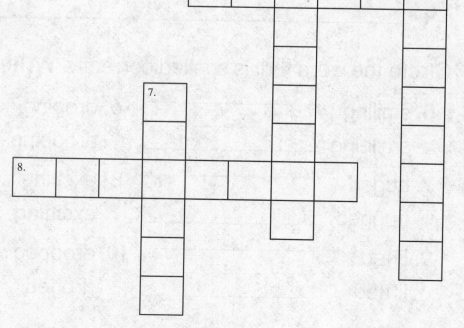

Home Activity Your child has been learning to spell words with -ed and -ing. Have your child circle the spelling words with double consonants (dropped, dropping, hugged, hugging).

Digraphs *ch, tch, sh, th, wh*

Generalization Some words have two or three consonants together that are said as one sound: <u>th</u>at, pa<u>tch</u>.

Sort the list words by **ch**, **tch**, **sh**, **th**, and **wh**.

tch

1. _____

2. _____

ch

3. _____

4. _____

sh

5. _____

6. _____

th

7. _____

8. _____

9. _____

wh

10. _____

11. _____

12. _____

Challenge Words
tch

13. _____

sh

15. _____

wh

14. _____

Spelling Words
1. bunch
2. that
3. wish
4. patch
5. when
6. what
7. math
8. them
9. shape
10. whale
11. itch
12. chase
Challenge Words
13. whiskers
14. switch
15. shrimp

School + Home

Home Activity Your child is learning to spell words with *ch, tch, sh, th,* and *wh.* To practice at home, have your child look at the word, pronounce it, write it, and then check it.

Digraphs *ch, tch, sh, th, wh*

Spelling Words					
bunch	that	wish	patch	when	what
math	them	shape	whale	itch	chase

Write a list word that rhymes.

1. fish _____

2. cape _____

3. male _____

4. lunch _____

5. base _____

6. bath _____

7. stem _____

8. pen _____

Write the missing words.

when	what
itch	patch
that	them

9. Did you hear _____ he said?

10. Does that bug bite _____ ?

11. He has a _____ on his eye.

12. I saw _____ movie.

Home Activity Your child spelled words with *ch, tch, sh, th,* and *wh*. Have your child circle these letter combinations in the spelling words.

Spelling Practice Book

Digraphs *ch, tch, sh, th, wh*

Read Mike's note. **Circle** three spelling mistakes. **Write** the words correctly. Then write the aunt's name correctly.

Dear aunt peg,
I whish you were here. We saw a whale. It had a white patch behind each eye. You can tell the male whale from the female whale by the shap of the fin. It was fun to wach.
Love, Mike

Spelling Words

bunch	math
that	them
wish	shape
patch	whale
when	itch
what	chase

Frequently Misspelled Words

when
watch
where

1. _____

2. _____

3. _____

4. _____

Fill in the circle to show the correct spelling. **Write** the word.

5. ○ ich   ○ itch   ○ itche   _____

6. ○ what   ○ whath   ○ waht   _____

7. ○ chas   ○ shaze   ○ chase   _____

8. ○ buntch   ○ bunsh   ○ bunch   _____

Home Activity Your child identified misspelled words with *ch, tch, sh, th,* and *wh.* Have your child write a pretend postcard using some of the words.

Name _____

Digraphs *ch, tch, sh, th, wh*

Unscramble the letters. **Write** the word.

	Spelling Words	
	bunch	math
	that	them
	wish	shape
	patch	whale
	when	itch
	what	chase

1. p e s a h   _____

2. c a s h e   _____

3. n e w h   _____

4. t a h m   _____

5. h i s w   _____

6. h l e w a   _____

7. c t h i   _____

Write list words to complete the tongue twisters.

8. Bev bought the best _____ of big beans.

9. Did _____ thin thief thank _____ ?

10. Please _____ pant pockets.

Home Activity Your child has been learning to spell words with *ch, tch, sh, th,* and *wh.* Help your child look for these letter combinations in the words on a calendar.

Spelling Practice Book

Words with *ar, or, ore*

Generalization The vowel sound /är/ is spelled **ar**: p<u>ar</u>t. The vowel sound /ôr/ can be spelled **or** and **ore**: b<u>or</u>n, m<u>ore</u>.

Sort the list words by *ar*, *or*, and *ore*.

ar	ore
1. _____	5. _____
2. _____	6. _____
3. _____	7. _____
4. _____	8. _____
or	
9. _____	10. _____
11. _____	12. _____

Challenge Words

ar	or
13. _____	14. _____
ore	
15. _____	

Spelling Words
1. part
2. hard
3. born
4. horse
5. before
6. more
7. smart
8. farm
9. porch
10. corn
11. chore
12. score
Challenge Words
13. cardinal
14. therefore
15. morning

Home Activity Your child is learning to spell words with *ar*, *or*, and *ore*. To practice at home, have your child look at the word, pronounce it, spell it aloud, and then write it.

Name _____

Words with *ar, or, ore*

Spelling Words					
part	hard	born	horse	before	more
smart	farm	porch	corn	chore	score

Add a list word to each group.

1. beans, peas, _____

2. city, town, _____

3. bright, clever, _____

4. pig, cow, _____

5. firm, solid, _____

6. door, roof, _____

7. piece, portion, _____

8. job, task, _____

Write the list word to finish each sentence.

9. I put on my socks _____ my shoes.

10. The _____ was 21 to 14.

11. The kittens were _____ last week.

12. May I have _____ pizza?

Home Activity Your child wrote words with *ar, or* and *ore*. Take turns with your child spelling the words and using them in sentences.

Spelling Practice Book

Words with *ar, or, ore*

Read Adam's article. Circle three spelling mistakes. Write the words correctly. Then write the sentence that does not belong.

Spelling Words	
part	smart
hard	farm
born	porch
horse	corn
before	chore
more	score

Second Grade News

Our Class Trip

Monday our class visited a farm. We fed corne to a hors. Tim is smart in math. A new colt was born just befor we got there.

1. _____ 2. _____

3. _____

4. _____

Frequently Misspelled Words

started

before

Write the underlined words correctly.

5. a high <u>scor</u> on a test
_____

6. sit on the <u>portch</u>
_____

7. a <u>partt</u> in the play
_____

8. <u>harde</u> as a rock
_____

9. <u>boren</u> last year
_____

10. <u>mor</u> than one
_____

Home Activity Your child has identified misspelled words with *ar, or* and *ore*. Ask your child to say the sound of each letter combination. (Note: The letter combinations *or* and *ore* have the same sound.)

Words with *ar, or, ore*

Spelling Words					
part	hard	born	horse	before	more
smart	farm	porch	corn	chore	score

Write a list word that rhymes with each word.

arm

1. _____

horn

2. _____

core

3. _____

torch

4. _____

store

5. _____

dart

6. _____

Write list words in the puzzle.

Down
7. task
9. not dumb

Across
8. ride a ____
10. not after

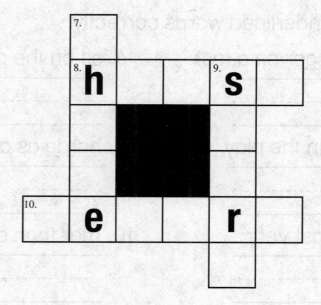

 Home Activity Your child has been learning to spell words with *ar, or,* and *ore*. Have your child pronounce the spelling words and underline *ar, or,* and *ore*.

Contractions

Generalization In contractions, an apostrophe (') takes the place of letters that are left out: **I will** becomes **I'll**.

Sort the list words by the word that has been shortened.

am

1. _____

not

2. _____

3. _____

4. _____

5. _____

6. _____

is or has

7. _____

8. _____

9. _____

10. _____

will

11. _____

12. _____

Challenge Words

is or has

13. _____

not

14. _____

15. _____

Spelling Words

1. I'll
2. wasn't
3. it's
4. he's
5. I'm
6. didn't
7. who's
8. she's
9. we'll
10. isn't
11. hasn't
12. hadn't

Challenge Words

13. wouldn't
14. shouldn't
15. where's

School + Home

Home Activity Your child is learning to spell contractions. To practice at home, have your child study the word, especially the placement of the apostrophe, and then spell the word.

Contractions

Spelling Words					
I'll	wasn't	it's	he's	I'm	didn't
who's	she's	we'll	isn't	hasn't	hadn't

Write the contraction that can be made from the underlined words.

1. The turtle <u>has not</u> come up for air.

2. It <u>is not</u> snowing.

3. Do you know <u>who is</u> riding the bus today?

4. I think <u>she is</u> at the nature center.

5. Tomorrow <u>we will</u> be at home.

6. The bird <u>was not</u> in the nest.

Write the contractions for the words below.

7. it is _____

8. did not _____

9. had not _____

10. I will _____

11. he is _____

12. I am _____

School + Home

Home Activity Your child wrote contractions. Have your child name the words that were combined to make each contraction.

Contractions

Spelling Words					
I'll	wasn't	it's	he's	I'm	didn't
who's	she's	we'll	isn't	hasn't	hadn't

Read Emmet's letter. Circle two spelling mistakes.
Circle the word with the capitalization mistake. Write
the words correctly.

Dear Grandpa,
Wasn't that a great game on friday?
I did't think you could come, but I'm
glad you did! Mom says its time for
dinner so I have to go.
Love, Emmet

1. _____

2. _____

3. _____

Fill in the circle to show the correct spelling.
Write the word.

4. ○ has't   ○ hasn't

5. ○ we'll   ○ we'ill

6. ○ she's   ○ shes

7. ○ whos'   ○ who's

8. ○ wasn't   ○ wan't

4. _____

5. _____

6. _____

7. _____

8. _____

Home Activity Your child identified misspelled contractions. Have your child point to each
apostrophe (') and tell what letter or letters the apostrophe replaced.

Contractions

Circle the correct word. Write it.

1. Do you think   its   it's   spicy?

   _____

   _____

2. He   had'nt   hadn't   finished.

   _____

3. I think   wel'l   we'll   buy it.

   _____

   _____

4. Do you know   who's   whos   coming?

   _____

   _____

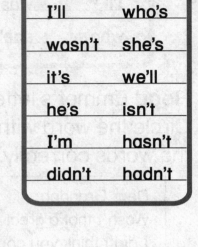

Spelling Words

I'll	who's
wasn't	she's
it's	we'll
he's	isn't
I'm	hasn't
didn't	hadn't

Circle the hidden list word. Write the word.

5. t m w a s n ' t e ' t r

   _____

   _____

6. e ' d i d n ' t o o s

   _____

   _____

7. m e ' r d h a s n ' t

   _____

   _____

8. I ' m m e x ' l l n l

   _____

   _____

9. s b d ' e d I ' l l o

   _____

   _____

10. f h i s n ' t e d ' s

    _____

    _____

School + Home

Home Activity Your child has been learning to spell contractions. Can your child think of other contractions that are not on the spelling list?

Name _____

Words with *er*, *ir*, *ur*

Generalization The vowel sound /ér/ can be spelled **er**, **ir**, or **ur**: her, nurse, dirt.

Sort the list words by **er**, **ir**, or **ur**:

er

1. _____

2. _____

3. _____

ir

4. _____

5. _____

6. _____

ur

7. _____

8. _____

9. _____

10. _____

11. _____

12. _____

Challenge Words

ur

13. _____

14. _____

er

15. _____

Spelling Words

1. her
2. person
3. nurse
4. dirt
5. turn
6. birth
7. serve
8. curb
9. curl
10. skirt
11. purse
12. turtle

Challenge Words

13. hamburger
14. surface
15. perfect

Home Activity Your child is learning to spell words with *er*, *ir*, and *ur*. To practice at home, have your child look at the word, say it, spell it, and then use the word in a sentence.

Spelling Practice Book

Unit 2 Week 3 **Day 1** **29**

Name _____

Words with *er*, *ir*, *ur*

Spelling Words					
her	person	nurse	dirt	turn	birth
serve	curb	curl	skirt	purse	turtle

Find two list words that fit the clues. **Write** them.

_____   _____

They have **ur**. They rhyme. 1. _____ 2. _____

They have **ir**. They rhyme. 3. _____ 4. _____

They have **ur**. They have **c**. 5. _____ 6. _____

Write the list word that fits each clue.

7. This person works with a doctor. 7. _____

8. This animal is a reptile. 8. _____

9. This is what waiters do. 9. _____

10. This is the opposite of him. 10. _____

11. This is what doorknobs do. 11. _____

12. It is when you were born. 12. _____

Home Activity Your child wrote words with *er*, *ir*, and *ur*. Have your child circle *er*, *ir*, and *ur* in the spelling words.

Name _____

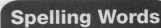

Words with *er*, *ir*, *ur*

Read Katie's form. **Circle** three spelling mistakes. **Circle** the word with a capitalization mistake. **Write** the words correctly.

Crafts Classes

Name of purson: <u>Katie Perez</u> Age: <u>7</u>

Check one: ☐ June camp ☐ july camp

Classes (first and second choice):

<u>My first choice is the clay tertle class.</u>

<u>My othur choice is the beaded purse class.</u>

Spelling Words

her	serve
person	curb
nurse	curl
dirt	skirt
turn	purse
birth	turtle

Frequently Misspelled Words

another

other

heard

were

1. _____

2. _____

3. _____

4. _____

Circle the word that is spelled correctly. **Write** it.

her	hir	hur	5. _____
skert	skirt	skurt	6. _____
nerse	nirse	nurse	7. _____
tern	tirn	turn	8. _____

School + Home

Home Activity Your child has identified misspelled words with *er*, *ir*, and *ur*. Remind your child that *er*, *ir*, and *ur* often have the same sound so each spelling word must be memorized.

Name _____

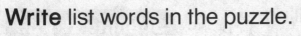

Words with *er*, *ir*, *ur*

Write list words in the puzzle.

Across

2. soil
5. handbag
6. human being

Spelling Words

her	serve
person	curb
nurse	curl
dirt	skirt
turn	purse
birth	turtle

Down

1. to work for
3. to change direction
4. to bend, twist, or roll

Write the word with the missing **er**, **ir**, or **ur**.

7. He is a kind p_ _son.

7. _____

8. What is your date of b_ _th?

8. _____

9. The t_ _tle was crossing the road.

9. _____

10. Abby shared h_ _ lunch with us.

10. _____

11. Did you get a t_ _n?

11. _____

12. I helped s_ _ve lunch.

12. _____

Home Activity Your child has been learning to spell words with *er, ir,* and *ur.* Look for these letter combinations in words in schoolbooks and library books.

Name _____

Adding -s and -es

Generalization Add **-s** to most words; add **-es** to words that end in **ch, sh,** or **x**; and change **y** to **i** and add **-es** to most words that end with **y**: note<u>s</u>, switch<u>es</u>, stor<u>ies</u>.

Sort according to how the plural is formed.

-s

1. _____

2. _____

3. _____

4. _____

-es

5. _____

6. _____

7. _____

8. _____

Change y to i add -es

9. _____

10. _____

11. _____

12. _____

Challenge Words

-s

13. _____

14. _____

Change y to i add -es

15. _____

Spelling Words
1. note
2. notes
3. lunch
4. lunches
5. story
6. stories
7. tune
8. tunes
9. switch
10. switches
11. baby
12. babies

Challenge Words

13. crumbs
14. supplies
15. holidays

School + Home

Home Activity Your child is learning to spell words with and without -s and -es. To practice at home, have your child say the word, write it, and then check it.

Spelling Practice Book

Unit 2 Week 4 **Day 1** **33**

Name _____

Adding -s and -es

Spelling Words					
note	lunch	story	tune	switch	baby
notes	lunches	stories	tunes	switches	babies

Write the missing list words.

1. I will eat my _____ now.

2. She told a _____ about a lost prince.

3. We packed _____ to eat on the hike.

4. My sister wrote two _____ .

5. Your _____ loves to eat bananas.

6. The _____ can play in the shade.

Write the list word that rhymes. Then write the word adding **-s** or **-es**.

dune	ditch	vote
_____	_____	_____
7. _____	8. _____	9. _____
10. _____	11. _____	12. _____

Home Activity Your child wrote words with and without -s and -es. Name a singular word and have your child explain how the plural is formed.

Spelling Practice Book

Adding -s and -es

Read the journal entry. **Circle** three spelling mistakes. **Circle** the word with a capitalization mistake. **Write** the words correctly.

Spelling Words

note	tune
notes	tunes
lunch	switch
lunches	switches
story	baby
stories	babies

My Journal

Monday
I ate lunch with my freinds. Then Mrs. perez read a story about a mother raccoon and her babys. I like storys.

Frequently Misspelled Words

friends

presents

1. _____ 2. _____

3. _____ 4. _____

Fill in the circle to show the correctly spelled word.

5. The ○ baby ○ beby ○ babys   is crying.

6. Turn the ○ switche ○ switch ○ swich   off.

7. Dad whistled some ○ tunes ○ tunies ○ tuns.

8. We can eat our ○ lunchs ○ lunches ○ lunchies   outside.

9. He wrote a ○ note ○ not ○ noties   to his friend.

10. The light ○ switchies ○ switchs ○ switches   are broken.

School + Home

Home Activity Your child has identified misspelled words with and without -s and -es. Ask your child to explain why -es is added to *lunch* and *switch*. (The words end with *ch*.)

Adding -s and -es

Spelling Words					
note	lunch	story	tune	switch	baby
notes	lunches	stories	tunes	switches	babies

Add a list word to each group.

change
shift
_____

1. _____

infant
child
_____

2. _____

brunch
dinner
_____

3. _____

melody
music
_____

4. _____

tale
book
_____

5. _____

letter
comment
_____

6. _____

Circle the **plural** of each of the words below
in the puzzle. The words may be across or down.

b l e s w i f h b j
a u s w i t c h e s
b s g n b n t s p r
i n o t e s e t m t
e w t c h k s o q u
s s e s a r n r l n
d n i e t i o i c e
l u n c h e s e h s
t o r y u n e s e b

lunch
switch
baby
notes
story
tune

Home Activity Your child has been learning to spell words with and without -s and -es. Spell a
singular spelling word and have your child spell the plural form. Then spell a plural word and have
your child spell the singular form.

Spelling Practice Book

Long *a*: *ai*, *ay*

Generalization Sometimes long **a** is spelled **ai** or **ay**: pail, day.

Sort the list words according to **ai** and **ay**.

ai	ay
1. _____	7. _____
2. _____	8. _____
3. _____	9. _____
4. _____	10. _____
5. _____	11. _____
6. _____	12. _____

Challenge Words

ai	ay
13. _____	15. _____
14. _____	

Spelling Words

1. tail
2. main
3. wait
4. say
5. away
6. play
7. raise
8. brain
9. paint
10. stay
11. today
12. tray

Challenge Words

13. holiday
14. daily
15. raisin

Home Activity Your child is learning to spell words with long *a* spelled *ai* and *ay*. To practice at home, have your child read each word to you. Say each word and ask your child to write the word on a piece of paper.

Name _____

Long a: ai, ay

Spelling Words					
tail	main	wait	say	away	play
raise	brain	paint	stay	today	tray

Write a list word to complete each phrase.

1. worth the _____   2. _____ the house

3. wag a _____   4. use your _____

5. _____ put   6. have the final _____

7. _____ the flag   8. _____ is the day

Write a list word to finish each sentence.

9. The bird flew _____ .

10. I can _____ after school.

11. Put your cup on the _____ .

12. The _____ road is closed.

School + Home

Home Activity Your child spelled words with long a spelled *ai* and *ay*. Ask your child to explain the meanings of the sayings on this page.

38 Unit 2 Week 5 **Day 2**   **Spelling Practice Book**

Name _____

Long *a*: *ai, ay*

Read the poster. **Circle** three spelling mistakes. **Write** the words correctly. Then write the last sentence, using correct grammar.

Fire Safety Tips

- Stay awai from fires.
- Replace worn electric cords because thay can start fires.
- Store paynt away from heat.
- Don't never play with matches.

1. _____
2. _____
3. _____

4. _____

Spelling Words

tail	raise
main	brain
wait	paint
say	stay
away	today
play	tray

Frequently Misspelled Words

favorite

they

Circle the word in each pair that is spelled correctly. **Write** the word.

5. tial
   tail
   _____

6. main
   mian
   _____

7. brain
   brian
   _____

8. raise
   rase
   _____

Home Activity Your child has been spelling words with long *a* spelled *ai* and *ay*. Have your child underline these letter combinations in the list words.

Long *a*: *ai*, *ay*

Spelling Words

tail	main	wait	say	away	play
raise	brain	paint	stay	today	tray

Draw a path through the maze. Follow the words that rhyme with *jay*. **Write** each word on the path.

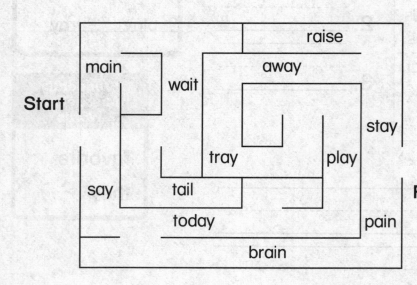

1. _____

2. _____

3. _____

4. _____

5. _____

6. _____

Write the words that fit each clue.

Two list words that end in **t**.

7. _____

8. _____

A list word that ends in **l**.

11. _____

Two list words that end in **n**.

9. _____

10. _____

A list word that ends in **e**.

12. _____

Home Activity Your child has been learning to spell words with long *a* spelled *ai* and *ay*. Take turns thinking of and spelling similar words.

Long e: ee, ea, y

Generalization Long e can be spelled ee, ea, and y: <u>fee</u>l, <u>easy</u>.

Sort the list words by **ee**, **ea**, and **y**.

ee

1. _____

2. _____

3. _____

4. _____

5. _____

ea and y

6. _____

ea

7. _____

8. _____

9. _____

10. _____

y

11. _____

12. _____

Challenge Words

13. _____

15. _____

ea

14. _____

Spelling Words
1. read
2. feel
3. easy
4. deep
5. seat
6. party
7. wheel
8. leave
9. windy
10. sleep
11. teeth
12. team
Challenge Words
13. wreath
14. season
15. eagle

School + Home **Home Activity** Your child is learning to spell words with long e: ee, ea, and y. To practice at home, have your child say the word, spell it, and then check it.

Long e: ee, ea, y

Spelling Words					
read	feel	easy	deep	seat	party
wheel	leave	windy	sleep	teeth	team

Write the missing list word. It rhymes with the name.

_____

1. Marty couldn't wait for the _____ .

_____

2. Mr. Peep went to _____ .

_____

3. Mrs. Steep dug a hole that is _____ .

_____

4. Mr. Heel asked, "How do you _____?"

_____

5. Cindy said that it was _____ .

_____

6. Mr. Snead likes to _____ .

_____

Write the list word that fits in each group.

_____

7. hood, bumper, _____   8. group, bunch, _____

9. chair, bench, _____   10. lips, tongue, _____

11. simple, basic, _____   12. go, depart, _____

Home Activity Your child spelled words with long e: *ee*, *ea*, and *y*. Have your child underline these
letter combinations in the list words.

Spelling Practice Book

Long e: *ee, ea, y*

Read Andy's note. **Circle** three spelling mistakes and an incorrect verb. **Write** the words correctly.

Spelling Words	
read	wheel
feel	leave
easy	windy
deep	sleep
seat	teeth
party	team

> Mom,
>
> I made the teem! The tryouts was easy. I have
> to leav bicause practice starts today. I'll be
> home for the party.
>
> Love, Andy

Frequently Misspelled Words

because

Easter

1. _____

2. _____

3. _____

4. _____

Fill in the circle to show the correct spelling.

5. ○ tethe   ○ teath   ○ teeth

6. ○ deap   ○ deep   ○ depe

7. ○ party   ○ partie   ○ partee

8. ○ rede   ○ reid   ○ read

9. ○ feal   ○ feel   ○ feil

10. ○ windy   ○ windey   ○ windie

Home Activity Your child identified misspelled words with long *e: ee, ea,* and *y*. Say a list word. Ask your child how the long *e* sound is spelled.

Spelling Practice Book

Unit 3 Week 1 **Day 3** **43**

Long e: ee, ea, y

Spelling Words

read	feel	easy	deep	seat	party
wheel	leave	windy	sleep	teeth	team

Write the missing list word to finish the sentence.

_____

1. It was very _____ at our campsite.

2. My _____ began to chatter.

3. I tried to get to _____ .

Write list words in the box below. The first letter of each word is shown.

seat read feel team wheel
leave party deep easy

4. **r** _____

5. **d** _____

6. **w** _____

7. **f** _____

8. **e** _____

9. **s** _____

10. **p** _____

11. **t** _____

12. **l** _____

Home Activity Your child has been learning to spell words with long e: ee, ea, and y. Put a dried bean (or other small object) on each word in the box on this page. Pronounce one of the words. Ask your child to spell it and win the bean. Continue with the other words.

Spelling Practice Book

Long o: o, oa, ow

Generalization Long **o** can be spelled **o**, **oa**, and **ow**: m<u>o</u>st, g<u>oa</u>t, b<u>ow</u>l.

Sort the list words by **o**, **oa**, and **ow**.

o

1. _____
2. _____
3. _____
4. _____
5. _____

oa

6. _____
7. _____
8. _____
9. _____

ow

10. _____
11. _____
12. _____

Challenge Words

o

13. _____

ow

14. _____

oa

15. _____

Spelling Words
1. goat
2. hold
3. show
4. most
5. bowl
6. float
7. toast
8. ago
9. open
10. told
11. toad
12. slow
Challenge Words
13. almost
14. throat
15. hollow

Home Activity Your child is learning to spell words with long *o* spelled *o*, *oa*, and *ow*. To practice at home, have your child spell each word. Then cover the word and ask them to spell it again.

Long o: o, oa, ow

Spelling Words					
goat	hold	show	most	bowl	float
toast	ago	open	told	toad	slow

Write two list words that rhyme with each word.

coat	gold	bow
1. _____	3. _____	5. _____
_____	_____	_____
2. _____	4. _____	6. _____

Write list words that mean almost the same thing as the underlined words.

7. He has the <u>largest number of</u> marbles.

_____

8. He moved here three years <u>back in time</u>.

_____

9. Put the apples in the <u>dish</u>.

_____

10. Shall I <u>brown</u> some bread for you?

_____

11. The <u>frog</u> jumped into the pond.

_____

12. The store is <u>not closed</u>.

_____

Home Activity Your child spelled words with long o spelled o, oa, and ow. Challenge your child to spell *bowl* and think of at least two different meanings for the word. (to knock down pins, a dish, a special football game)

Spelling Practice Book

Name _____

Long o: o, oa, ow

Read Carrie's letter. **Circle** three spelling mistakes and one word with a capitalization error. **Write** the words correctly.

Dear Sir:

   My family tried Corny Puffs a few days ago. We got the box opin, but most of the Corny Puffs were gone. we only could fill one bowl. I had to eat tost.

   I no you will want to send us a new, full box.

Thank you,

Carrie

Spelling Words	
goat	toast
hold	ago
show	open
most	told
bowl	toad
float	slow

Frequently Misspelled Words

Halloween

know

1. _____   2. _____

3. _____   4. _____

Circle the correct word. **Write** it.

5. gowt goat   _____

6. hoald hold   _____

7. slow slo   _____

8. flowt float   _____

9. bowl bowal   _____

10. show sho   _____

Home Activity Your child identified misspelled words with long o spelled o, oa, and ow. Have your child underline these letter combinations in the list words.

Long *o*: *o*, *oa*, *ow*

Spelling Words					
goat	hold	show	most	bowl	float
toast	ago	open	told	toad	slow

Read the clue. **Write** the list word.

Add a letter to **low** to make a word that means **not fast**.

Add a letter to **how** to make a word that means a **movie**.

1. _____

2. _____

Add a letter to **bow** to make a word that means **dish**.

Add a letter to **old** to make a word that means **hang onto something**.

3. _____

4. _____

Read the clues. **Write** the list words. The word in the boxes will answer the riddle.

What has eyes, but can't see?

5. You do this to a window.   __ __ __ __

6. This is the opposite of least.   __ __ __ __

7. This animal has no tail.   __ __ __ __

8. An animal with horns and beard. __ __ __ __

9. You eat this for breakfast.   __ __ __ __ __

10. You can do this in the water. __ __ __ __

Home Activity Your child has been learning to spell words with long *o* spelled *o*, *oa*, and *ow*. Give clues about a list word. Challenge your child to guess and spell it.

Compound Words

Generalization A compound word is made up of two other words:
some + one = someone.

Sort the list words by whether or not you know
how to spell them. **Write** every word.

Copyright © Savvas Learning Company LLC. All Rights Reserved.

words I know how to spell	words I'm learning to spell
1. _____	7. _____
2. _____	8. _____
3. _____	9. _____
4. _____	10. _____
5. _____	11. _____
6. _____	12. _____

Spelling Words

1. basketball
2. someone
3. weekend
4. something
5. birthday
6. riverbank
7. bathtub
8. backyard
9. driveway
10. bedtime
11. raindrop
12. mailbox

Challenge Words

13. grandparent
14. rattlesnake
15. earthquake

Challenge Words

words I know how to spell	words I'm learning to spell
13. _____	15. _____
14. _____	

Home Activity Your child is learning to spell compound words. To practice at home, have your
child study the word and its parts, spell the word with eyes closed, and then write the word.

Compound Words

Spelling Words					
basketball	someone	weekend	something	birthday	riverbank
bathtub	backyard	driveway	bedtime	raindrop	mailbox

Write a list word to name each picture.

1. _____

2. _____

3. _____

4. _____

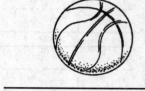

5. _____

6. _____

Write the list word that can be made by joining the two words together.

week + end

7. _____

some + one

8. _____

back + yard

9. _____

river + bank

10. _____

bed + time

11. _____

some + thing

12. _____

Home Activity Your child spelled compound words. Ask your child to name the small words in each compound word.

Compound Words

Read the journal entry. **Circle** three spelling mistakes. **Write** the words correctly. Then write the second sentence, using the correct verb.

Here's what happened on my birth day. Dad says to go owtside. I might find something in the driveway. It was a basketbal hoop! I played ball until bedtime.

Spelling Words

basketball	bathtub
someone	backyard
weekend	driveway
something	bedtime
birthday	raindrop
riverbank	mailbox

1. _____

2. _____

3. _____

4. _____

Frequently Misspelled Words

outside

everybody

sometimes

baseball

Compound Names Circle and write the list word that is spelled correctly.

5. You need to hop in the **bath tub / bathtub**. _____

6. We sat on the **riverbank / rivorbank**. _____

7. I found a postcard in the **mailbox / malebox**. _____

8. We will play in the **bakyard / backyard**. _____

School + Home

Home Activity Your child identified misspelled compound words. Have your child spell the parts of each compound word separately.

Compound Words

Spelling Words					
basketball	someone	weekend	something	birthday	riverbank
bathtub	backyard	driveway	bedtime	raindrop	mailbox

Connect the parts. **Write** the word.

1. bath   yard   1. _____

2. river   tub   2. _____

3. back   ball   3. _____

4. basket   thing   4. _____

5. some   bank   5. _____

Write the words in the box in ABC order.

6. _____   10. _____

7. _____   11. _____

8. _____   12. _____

9. _____

someone
weekend
birthday
driveway
raindrop
mailbox
bedtime

School + Home

Home Activity Your child has been learning to spell compound words. Help your child brainstorm other compound words.

Long *i*: *i*, *igh*, *y*

Generalization Long **i** can be spelled **i**, **igh**, and **y**: **find**, **right**, **fly**.

Sort the list words according to **i**, **igh**, and **y**.

Spelling Words
1. find
2. child
3. sky
4. bright
5. wild
6. fly
7. right
8. flight
9. spider
10. cry
11. blind
12. myself
Challenge Words
13. frighten
14. arrival
15. identify

i

1. _____

2. _____

3. _____

4. _____

5. _____

igh

6. _____

7. _____

8. _____

y

9. _____

10. _____

11. _____

12. _____

Challenge Words

i

13. _____

igh

14. _____

i and y

15. _____

School + Home

Home Activity Your child is learning to spell words with long *i*: *i*, *igh*, and *y*. To practice at home, write each word, say it and circle the long *i* sound.

Name _____

Long *i*: *i*, *igh*, *y*

Spelling Words					
find	child	sky	bright	wild	fly
right	flight	spider	cry	blind	myself

Write a list word to finish the comparison.

1. hear and deaf, _____

   see and _____

2. moon and dim, _____

   sun and _____

3. six legs and ant, _____

   eight legs and _____

4. bad and good, _____

   wrong and _____

5. happy and laugh, _____

   sad and _____

6. dog and run, _____

   bird and _____

7. old and grandparent, _____

   young and _____

8. dog and tame, _____

   tiger and _____

Write a list word to finish each phrase.

9. me, _____ , and I

10. _____ the treasure

11. take _____

12. blue _____

Home Activity Your child spelled words with long *i*: *i*, *igh*, and *y*. Have your child choose a number between á and áé. Ask your child to spell the word with that item number on this page.

54 Unit 3 Week 4 **Day 2**

Spelling Practice Book

Name _____

Long *i*: *i*, *igh*, *y*

Read Jill's weather report. **Circle** three spelling mistakes. **Write** the words correctly. Then write the correct form of the verb that is underlined.

Right now, we have rain with some wild winds. Airplanes can't fli. By noon, the skigh will clear. It will be warm, and the sun <u>is</u> bright. We mite still have some light wind.

Spelling Words	
find	right
child	flight
sky	spider
bright	cry
wild	blind
fly	myself

1. _____

2. _____

3. _____

4. _____

Frequently Misspelled Words

might

I

Fill in the circle to show the correct word.
Write the word.

_____

5. His dog is almost ◯ bline ◯ blind .

_____

6. Hit the ball with your ◯ right ◯ rite hand.

_____

7. I can plant the seeds ◯ myself ◯ mighself.

_____

8. There's a ◯ spyder ◯ spider in the corner. _____

Home Activity Your child has been spelling words with long *i*: *i*, *igh*, and *y*. Ask your child to find examples of list words with these letter combinations.

Spelling Practice Book   Unit 3 Week 4 **Day 3** **55**

Long *i: i, igh, y*

Spelling Words

find	child	sky	bright	wild	fly
right	flight	spider	cry	blind	myself

Read the two words. **Write** a list word that would come between them in a dictionary.

1. lungs _____ nice   2. fast _____ flame

3. water _____ yard   4. boat _____ chill

5. pull _____ run   6. apple _____ can

Unscramble each word. **Write** the word.

7. kys _____   8. glihft _____

9. tibrhg _____   10. yrc _____

11. ripsde _____   12. lyf _____

Home Activity Your child has been learning to spell word with long *i: i, igh,* and *y.* Have your child point to and read words that have a long *i* sound in exercises 1 to 6.

Adding -*er* and -*est*

Generalization When adding -**er** and -**est**, some base words do not change: soon<u>er</u>, soon<u>est</u>. Others do change: bus<u>ier</u>, bus<u>iest</u>, fa<u>tter</u>, fa<u>ttest</u>.

Sort the list words by -**er** and -**est**.

Spelling Words
1. sooner
2. soonest
3. hotter
4. hottest
5. busier
6. busiest
7. happier
8. happiest
9. smaller
10. smallest
11. fatter
12. fattest
Challenge Words
13. angrier
14. angriest
15. straighter
16. straightest

-er

1. _____

2. _____

3. _____

4. _____

5. _____

6. _____

-est

7. _____

8. _____

9. _____

10. _____

11. _____

12. _____

Challenge Words

-er

13. _____

14. _____

-est

15. _____

16. _____

Home Activity Your child is learning to spell words with -*er* and -*est*. To practice at home, ask your child to point out which base words change when adding -*er* and -*est*.

Adding -er and -est

Spelling Words					
sooner	soonest	hotter	hottest	busier	busiest
happier	happiest	smaller	smallest	fatter	fattest

Draw a line to connect the rule for adding **-er** and **-est** to the base word. **Write** the **-er** and **-est** word.

Double the final consonant.

Change y to i.

Do nothing to the base word.

soon 1. _____ 2. _____

fat 3. _____ 4. _____

busy 5. _____ 6. _____

Add -er or **-est** to the underlined word. **Write** the word.

7. Today is <u>hot</u> than Tuesday. _____

8. This child is the <u>happy</u> one in the play group. _____

9. These are the <u>small</u> muffins I've ever seen. _____

10. She is <u>happy</u> than she used to be. _____

11. This is the <u>hot</u> day of the year. _____

12. My cat is <u>small</u> than your cat. _____

Home Activity Your child spelled words with *-er* and *-est*. Ask your child to name other list words that follow each rule.

Spelling Practice Book

Name _____

Adding *-er* and *-est*

Read Sara's travel tips. **Circle** three spelling mistakes. **Circle** the word with a capitalization mistake. **Write** the words correctly.

Traveling with Pets

🐾 Everyone will be happyer and safer if Fido rides in a pet carrier.

🐾 Take breaks sooner than usual. Let your pet exercise and get a drink.

🐾 One of the hotest spots is a closed car in the sun. don't leave your pet their!

Spelling Words	
sooner	happier
soonest	happiest
hotter	smaller
hottest	smallest
busier	fatter
busiest	fattest

Frequently Misspelled Words

there

their

1. _____

2. _____

3. _____

4. _____

Circle the correctly spelled word. Write it.

5. busyiest
   busiest _____

6. fatest
   fattest _____

7. smaller
   smallier _____

8. sonnest
   soonest _____

9. fatter
   fater _____

10. busier
    busyer _____

Home Activity Your child identified misspelled words with *-er* and *-est*. Pronounce a list word with *-er*. Ask your child to spell the *-est* word.

Name _____

Adding -er and -est

Spelling Words					
sooner	soonest	hotter	hottest	busier	busiest
happier	happiest	smaller	smallest	fatter	fattest

Write **-er** words across and **-est** words down.

Across: Write the **-er** form of the word.

  2. busy   **4.** happy
  7. soon   **8.** small

Down: Write the **-est** form of the word.

  I. fat   **3.** small
  5. hot   **6.** happy

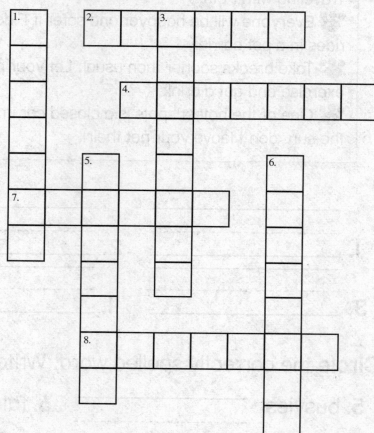

Circle the hidden list words.
Write the word.

9. s h o t t e r o o e s t

_____

10. s o b u s i e s t t e r

_____

II. b u f a t r f a t t e r

_____

12. h o t s o o n e s t e r

_____

Home Activity Your child has been learning to spell words with *-er* and *-est*. Help your child think of and spell other *-er* and *-est* words.

60 Unit 3 Week 5 **Day 4**

Spelling Practice Book

Name _____

Words Ending in -*le*

Generalization The syllable pattern in the final syllable of *apple* is often spelled **-le**.

Sort the list words by whether or not you know how to spell them. Write every word.

words I know how to spell

_____

1. _____

2. _____

3. _____

4. _____

5. _____

6. _____

words I'm learning to spell

_____

7. _____

8. _____

9. _____

10. _____

11. _____

12. _____

Spelling Words

1. ankle
2. title
3. apple
4. cable
5. purple
6. able
7. bugle
8. bundle
9. bubble
10. giggle
11. sparkle
12. tickle

Challenge Words

13. mumble
14. scramble
15. twinkle

Challenge Words

words I know how to spell

_____

13. _____

words I'm learning to spell

_____

14. _____

15. _____

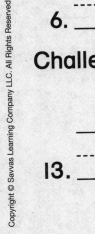

Home Activity Your child is learning to spell words that end in -*le*. To practice at home, have your child read the words in both lists. Have them spell the words they are learning to spell. Then have them spell all of the list words.

Name _____

Words Ending in *-le*

Spelling Words					
ankle	title	apple	cable	purple	able
bugle	bundle	bubble	giggle	sparkle	tickle

Use a list word to complete each phrase.

_____   _____

1. _____ of my eye   2. burst your _____

3. _____ up   4. strong and _____

5. book _____   6. sprain an _____

Write a list word to answer the riddle.

It rhymes with **wiggle**. It starts like **gate**.

It rhymes with **stable**. It starts like **can**.

It rhymes with **pickle**. It starts like **tent**.

7. _____   8. _____   9. _____

Write the missing word.

10. He plays the _____ .

11. I like the color _____ .

12. The stars in the sky shine and _____ .

Home Activity Your child spelled words that end with *-le*. Ask your child to explain the meanings of the popular sayings on this page.

Name _____

Words Ending in *-le*

Read the directions. **Circle** two spelling mistakes. **Write** the words correctly. **Rewrite** Step 4 as two sentences.

> **Are You Able to Make a Book?**
> 1. Stack six sheets of white paper. Use less if you want to make a litle book.
> 2. Put a sheet of colored paper on top. Use purpil or your favorite color.
> 3. Staple the book together on the left.
> 4. Put a title on the cover, write a story on the white pages.

Spelling Words

ankle	bugle
title	bundle
apple	bubble
cable	giggle
purple	sparkle
able	tickle

Frequently Misspelled Words

people

little

1. _____   2. _____

3. _____

Fill in the circle to show the correctly spelled word.

4. ○ ankel   ○ ankl   ○ ankle
5. ○ giggle   ○ gigle   ○ giggel
6. ○ sparkel   ○ sparkle   ○ sparkal
7. ○ bundal   ○ bundel   ○ bundle
8. ○ bugel   ○ bugl   ○ bugle

Home Activity Your child identified misspelled words that end with *-le*. Your child may enjoy following the directions at the top of the page to assemble and write a book.

Name _____

Words Ending in *-le*

Spelling Words					
ankle	title	apple	cable	purple	able
bugle	bundle	bubble	giggle	sparkle	tickle

Read a clue and write the list word. When you have written all six words, the answer to the riddle will appear in the boxes.

I go out each day, but never leave my home. What am I?

1. above the foot ☐ _ _ _ _ _

2. shine ☐ _ _ _ _ _ _

3. package _ _ ☐ _ _ _

4. a kind of fruit ☐ _ _ _ _

5. name of a book _ _ ☐ _ _

6. skillful _ ☐ _ _

Cross out all of these letters: **s, w, a, m, p.**
Write a list word by copying the letters that are left.

7. s t i a c w k l p e

    _____

    _____

8. a g i p g g s s l e

    _____

    _____

9. m b u a g p l m e

    _____

    _____

10. b u b w b m l e p

    _____

    _____

Home Activity Your child has been learning to spell words that end with *-le*. Give clues about a list word. Ask your child to guess and spell the word.

Spelling Practice Book

Vowel Sound in *book*

Generalization The vowel sound in *book* can be spelled **oo** and **u**: c<u>oo</u>k, p<u>u</u>t.

Sort the list words by **oo** or **u**.

oo	u
_____	_____
1. _____	8. _____
2. _____	9. _____
3. _____	10. _____
4. _____	11. _____
5. _____	12. _____
6. _____	
7. _____	

Spelling Words

1. put
2. cook
3. stood
4. full
5. wood
6. July
7. shook
8. push
9. pull
10. brook
11. hook
12. hood

Challenge Words

13. pudding
14. cushion
15. footprint

Challenge Words

oo	u
_____	_____
13. _____	14. _____
	15. _____

Home Activity Your child is learning words with the vowel sound in book spelled *oo* and *u*. To practice at home, ask your child to say each word. Then ask them to use each word in a sentence. Encourage your child to make sentences using more than one list word.

Vowel Sound in *book*

Spelling Words					
put	cook	stood	full	wood	July
shook	push	pull	brook	hook	hood

Write a list word that rhymes with the underlined word.

_____

1. Where does Alexa <u>look</u> for stones?   _____

_____

2. What did Bob wear to keep <u>good</u> and dry?   _____

_____

3. Sam <u>took</u> it fishing.   _____

_____

4. Who was reading the <u>book</u>?   _____

Read the word. **Write** a related list word.

_____   _____

5. June: _____   6. empty: _____

7. tug: _____   8. set: _____

9. pull: _____   10. shake: _____

11. sat: _____   12. chair: _____

Home Activity Your child wrote words with the vowel sound in *book* spelled *oo* and *u*. Pronounce a list word. Ask your child if the vowel sound is spelled *oo* or *u*.

Vowel Sound in *book*

Circle two spelling mistakes. **Circle** the word with the capitalization mistake. **Write** the words correctly.

Spelling Words	
put	shook
cook	push
stood	pull
full	brook
wood	hook
July	hood

Helper Wanted
Have you cooked out alot?
Can you cook on a wud fire?
Help younger campers cook.
camp begins on July 7.

1. _____

2. _____

3. _____

Fill in the circle to show the correctly spelled word. **Write** the word.

Frequently Misspelled Words
took
a lot

4. ○ stede   ○ stude   ○ stood   _____

5. ○ hud   ○ hood   ○ hude   _____

6. ○ push   ○ poosh   ○ pash   _____

7. ○ july   ○ Jully   ○ July   _____

8. ○ brock   ○ brook   ○ bruck   _____

9. ○ hook   ○ ohok   ○ ohoke   _____

10. ○ oshuk   ○ osook   ○ shook   _____

Home Activity Your child identified misspelled words with the vowel sound in *book* spelled *oo* and *u*. Have your child underline oo and u in the list words.

Vowel Sound in *book*

Spelling Words					
put	cook	stood	full	wood	July
shook	push	pull	brook	hook	hood

Fill each box with list words that rhyme.

book

1. _____

2. _____

3. _____

4. _____

good

5. _____

6. _____

7. _____

Find the list words in the box in the puzzle. Look across, down, and diagonally. **Circle** the words.

```
k  p  u  l  l  j  t
p  a  z  f  u  l  l
u  o  p  h  s  x  u
s  k  u  w  o  u  d
h  h  t  u  p  o  g
d  w  J  u  l  y  k
```

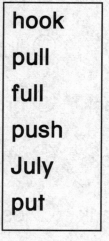

hook
pull
full
push
July
put

School + Home

Home Activity Your child has been learning to spell words with the vowel sound in *book* spelled *oo* and *u*. Take turns thinking of and spelling similar words.

Name _____

Vowel Sound in *gown*

Generalization The vowel sound in *gown* can be spelled **ou** and **ow**: s**ou**nd, fl**ow**er.

Sort the list words by **ou** or **ow**.

ou	ow
_____	_____

1. _____
2. _____
3. _____
4. _____
5. _____
6. _____
7. _____

8. _____
9. _____
10. _____
11. _____
12. _____

Spelling Words
1. around
2. about
3. gown
4. sound
5. flower
6. howl
7. ground
8. pound
9. crown
10. south
11. mouse
12. downtown
Challenge Words
13. mountain
14. boundary
15. drowsy

Challenge Words

ou	ow
_____	_____

13. _____
14. _____

15. _____

Home Activity Your child is learning to spell words with the vowel sound in *gown* spelled *ou* and *ow*. To practice at home, have your child study the word, write it, cover it, and then write it again.

Vowel Sound in *gown*

Spelling Words					
around	about	gown	sound	flower	howl
ground	pound	crown	south	mouse	downtown

Write a list word to complete each phrase.

_____   _____

1. _____ the corner   2. the king's _____

3. a house _____   4. _____ the same

5. a _____ pot   6. shop _____

Read the clue. **Write** the list word.

7. the same as soil   _____

8. the opposite of north   _____

9. the same as to hit   _____

10. the opposite of silence   _____

11. the same as to yell   _____

12. the same as dress   _____

Home Activity Your child wrote words with the vowel sound in *gown* spelled *ou* and *ow*. Have your child circle *ou* and *ow* in the list words.

Vowel Sound in *gown*

Read the story. **Circle** three spelling mistakes. Then circle a word with a capitalization error. **Write** the words correctly.

Pedro

There once was a mouse with wings. He was named Pedro. Usually Pedro lived on the ground near a little yellow hous.
In the fall, Pedro flew sowth to mexico.
There, he slept under a flowr.

Spelling Words	
around	ground
about	pound
gown	crown
sound	south
flower	mouse
howl	downtown

I. _____

2. _____

3. _____

4. _____

Frequently Misspelled Words

found

about

house

our

Read the sentence. **Circle** the correctly spelled word.

5. I need a _____ of butter.   **pound**   **pownd**

6. They will _____ with laughter.   **howl**   **houl**

7. Did you hear _____ the quiz?   **abowt**   **about**

8. What was that_____?   **sound**   **sownd**

9. Her party _____ is pretty.   **goun**   **gown**

10. We took the train _____.   **downtown**   **dountown**

Home Activity Your child identified misspelled words with the vowel sound in *gown* spelled *ou* and *ow*. Have your child use list words to tell more about Pedro's adventures.

Name _____

Vowel Sound in *gown*

Spelling Words					
around	about	gown	sound	flower	howl
ground	pound	crown	south	mouse	downtown

Read the clues. **Write** the word. Do not use any word more than once.

It has six letters. It rhymes with power. 1. _____	It has five letters. It rhymes with town. 2. _____	It rhymes with frown. It starts with g. 3. _____
It starts with p. It rhymes with found. 4. _____	It rhymes with mound. It starts with a. 5. _____	It has six letters. It starts with g. 6. _____
It starts with s. It rhymes with round. 7. _____	It starts with s. It rhymes with mouth. 8. _____	It has four letters. It starts with h. 9. _____

Unscramble each word.

10. t a u o b _____

11. s m e o u _____

12. w w o o d n n t _____

Home Activity Your child has been learning to spell words with the vowel sound in *gown* spelled *ou* and *ow*. Have your child pick a number between á and áê. Pronounce the word on this page with that number. Can your child spell the word?

Spelling Practice Book

Name _____

Vowel Sound in *joy*

Generalization The vowel sound in *joy* can be spelled **oi** and **oy**: n**oi**se, r**oy**al.

Sort the list words by **oi** or **oy**.

oi	oy
1.	7.
2.	8.
3.	9.
4.	10.
5.	11.
6.	12.

Challenge Words

oi	oy
13.	14.
	15.

Spelling Words

1. joy
2. noise
3. royal
4. moist
5. broil
6. cowboy
7. spoil
8. joint
9. foil
10. enjoy
11. destroy
12. loyal

Challenge Words

13. employee
14. corduroy
15. turquoise

School + Home

Home Activity Your child is learning to spell words with the vowel sound in *joy* spelled *oi* and *oy*. To practice at home, have your child study the word, spell it aloud, and then write it.

Name _____

Vowel Sound in *joy*

Spelling Words					
joy	noise	royal	moist	broil	cowboy
spoil	joint	foil	enjoy	destroy	loyal

Write a list word that rhymes with the underlined word.

1. <u>Roy</u> has a _____ hat.

2. The _____ dog had a <u>royal</u> blue collar.

3. I'll cover this with _____ so it doesn't <u>soil</u>.

4. Everyone was <u>loyal</u> to the _____ family.

5. Brush <u>oil</u> on the meat before you _____ it.

6. One of the _____ owners can <u>point</u> out the boat.

Write the list word that means the opposite.

7. silence _____

8. protect _____

9. dry _____

10. sadness _____

11. dislike _____

12. build _____

Home Activity Your child spelled words with the vowel sound in joy spelled *oi* and *oy*. Have your child underline *oi* and *oy* in the list words.

Spelling Practice Book

Vowel Sound in *joy*

Read about the life of a cowboy. **Circle** three spelling mistakes. **Write** the words correctly. Then write the correct form of **sing**.

Spelling Words	
joy	spoil
noise	joint
royal	foil
moist	enjoy
broil	destroy
cowboy	loyal

Cowboys took care of cattle. There were no fences, so each year the cattle were branded. The brand showed who owned the cattle. Branding was a joynt effort. At night, the cowboys would injoy sing around a fire. Fewer cowboys were needed wonce fences came into use.

Frequently Misspelled Words
one
once
first

1. _____
2. _____
3. _____
4. _____

Circle the list word that is spelled correctly.

5. noise   noyze
6. moist   miost

7. destroy   distroy
8. lowal   loyal

9. ryoal   royal
10. broal   broil

11. joiy   joy
12. foyl   foil

Home Activity Your child has identified misspelled words with the vowel sound in *joy* spelled *oi* and *oy*. Take turns with your child pointing to and spelling the list words.

Spelling Practice Book   Unit 4 Week 4 **Day 3**   75

Vowel Sound in *joy*

Spelling Words

joy	noise	royal	moist	broil	cowboy
spoil	joint	foil	enjoy	destroy	loyal

Write the missing list words to complete the puzzle.

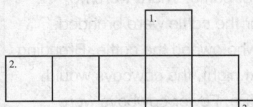

Across
2. be happy
3. thin sheet of metal
5. ruin
6. grill

Down
1. sounds
4. faithful

Write a list word that would come between the two words in a dictionary.

7. say _____ table

8. lunch _____ must

9. egg _____ fast

10. finish _____ joke

Home Activity Your child has been learning to spell words with the vowel sound in *joy* spelled *oi* and *oy*. Ask your child how all the words are the same. (All have the vowel sound found in *joy*, all have *o*, all have *oi* or *oy*.)

Spelling Practice Book

Vowel Sound in *moon*

Generalization The vowel sound in *moon* can be spelled **oo**, **ue**, **ew**, and **ui**:
t<u>oo</u>, bl<u>ue</u>, n<u>ew</u>, fr<u>ui</u>t.

Sort the list words by **oo**, **ue**, **ew**, and **ui**.

oo
_____

1. _____

2. _____

3. _____

ue
_____

4. _____

5. _____

6. _____

ew
_____

7. _____

8. _____

9. _____

ui
_____

10. _____

11. _____

12. _____

Challenge Words

oo
_____

13. _____

ew
_____

15. _____

ui
_____

14. _____

Spelling Words
1. too
2. new
3. fruit
4. blue
5. true
6. cool
7. suit
8. spoon
9. clue
10. juice
11. drew
12. flew
Challenge Words
13. cruise
14. nephew
15. shampoo

Home Activity Your child is learning words with the vowel sound in *moon* spelled *oo*, *ue*, *ew*, and *ui*. To practice at home, have your child study the word, noting the spelling of the vowel sound, and then write the word.

Vowel Sound in *moon*

Spelling Words					
too	new	fruit	blue	true	cool
suit	spoon	clue	juice	drew	flew

Write a list word that means the same as the underlined word.

1. Can I play <u>also</u>?

1. _____

2. He <u>painted</u> a picture.

2. _____

3. Is it <u>correct</u> that we tied?

3. _____

4. Let's start a <u>fresh</u> game.

4. _____

Add a list word to each group.

5. milk, water, _____

6. red, yellow, _____

7. soup, bread, _____

8. dress, skirt, _____

9. fork, knife, _____

10. ran, swam, _____

11. warm, cold, _____

12. tip, hint, _____

Home Activity Your child spelled words with the vowel sound in *moon* spelled *oo, ue, ew,* and *ui.* Have your child point out these letter combinations in the list words.

Spelling Practice Book

Vowel Sound in *moon*

Read the invitation. **Circle** two spelling mistakes. **Circle** a word with a capitalization error. **Write** the words correctly.

Please come too the class picnic Saturday at 4:00. The menu includes hot dogs, fruit salad, and jiuce. bring your own plate, fork, and spoon.

Spelling Words	
too	suit
new	spoon
fruit	clue
blue	juice
true	drew
cool	flew

1. _____ 2. _____ 3. _____

Fill in the circle next to the word that is spelled correctly. **Write** the word.

Frequently Misspelled Words

too   to
two

4. ○ clew   ○ clue   ○ clui   _____

5. ○ trew   ○ true   ○ tru   _____

6. ○ floo   ○ fue   ○ flew   _____

7. ○ cool   ○ cul   ○ cewl   _____

8. ○ bluw   ○ bloo   ○ blue   _____

9. ○ suit   ○ sute   ○ siut   _____

10. ○ drew   ○ dru   ○ drue   _____

School + Home

Home Activity Your child has identified misspelled words with the vowel sound in *moon* spelled *oo, ue, ew,* and *ui*. Have your child identify and spell one or more words with each of these letter combinations.

Vowel Sound in *moon*

Draw a line through three rhyming words in a row. Look across, down, and diagonally. **Write** the words.

flew	juice	spoon
lawn	new	fruit
suit	cool	drew

fruit	cool	clue
spoon	paw	blue
juice	suit	true

Spelling Words	
too	suit
new	spoon
fruit	clue
blue	juice
true	drew
cool	flew

1. _____

2. _____

3. _____

4. _____

5. _____

6. _____

Circle the list word that is hidden in the puzzle. **Write** it.

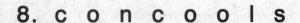

7. k j u i c e l o   _____

8. c o n c o o l s   _____

9. i n s p o o n e   _____

10. s t o o r e l   _____

11. l e s u i t e b   _____

12. c o f r u i t s   _____

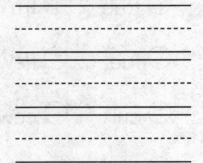

School + Home **Home Activity** Your child has been learning to spell words with the vowel sound in *moon* spelled *oo*, *ue*, *ew*, and *ui*. Create hidden words like those in Exercises 7–12 and have your child circle the list words.

Suffixes -*ly*, -*ful*, -*er*, -*or*

Generalization When suffixes **-ly**, **-ful**, **-er**, and **-or** are added to most words, the base word stays the same.

Sort the list words by their suffixes.

Spelling Words
1. cheerful
2. visitor
3. slowly
4. weekly
5. teacher
6. helper
7. hardly
8. graceful
9. yearly
10. quickly
11. fighter
12. sailor

-ly

1. _____

2. _____

3. _____

4. _____

5. _____

-ful

6. _____

7. _____

-er

8. _____

9. _____

10. _____

-or

11. _____

12. _____

Challenge Words

-ly

13. _____

-er

14. _____

-or

15. _____

Challenge Words
13. gardener
14. competitor
15. extremely

Home Activity Your child is learning to spell words with the suffixes -*ly*, -*ful*, -*er*, and -*or*. To practice at home, have your child point to each base word. Then have them say the base word and the base word with the suffix.

Suffixes *-ly*, *-ful*, *-er*, *-or*

Spelling Words

cheerful	visitor	slowly	weekly	teacher	helper
hardly	graceful	yearly	quickly	fighter	sailor

Write a list word that means the same as each phrase.

someone who teaches   every 365 days   someone who helps

_____   _____   _____

1. _____   2. _____   3. _____

someone who fights   someone who sails   full of happiness

_____   _____   _____

4. _____   5. _____   6. _____

Write list words that mean the same as the underlined words.

_____

7. We meet <u>every seven days</u>.   _____

8. We have a <u>guest</u>.   _____

9. The turtle moves <u>with little speed</u>.   _____

10. I <u>barely</u> had time to finish.   _____

11. She walks <u>rapidly</u>.   _____

12. The dancer is <u>not awkward</u>.   _____

Home Activity Your child spelled words with the suffixes *-ly*, *-ful*, *-er*, and *-or*. Point to a word. Ask your child to identify the suffix and spell the word.

Suffixes *-ly, -ful, -er, -or*

Spelling Words					
cheerful	visitor	slowly	weekly	teacher	helper
hardly	graceful	yearly	quickly	fighter	sailor

Read about Tracy's job. **Circle** three spelling mistakes. **Write** the words correctly. Then write the last sentence using correct grammar.

Frequently Misspelled Words

beautiful

through

I am the music helpar. We have music class weekly. I help the teecher pass out song sheets and instruments. I put things away when we are threw. I works quickly.

1. _____ 2. _____ 3. _____

4. _____

Circle the word that is spelled correctly.

5. I can get ready _____.   quickly   quickle

6. Who was your _____?   visiter   visitor

7. The _____ cleaned the deck.   sailor   sailer

8. It _____ ever snows there.   hardly   hardlie

9. We saw a _____ plane.   fightor   fighter

10. This is a _____ room.   cheerfull   cheerful

Home Activity Ask your child to name the three words they find the most difficult. Have your child divide each word and spell the base word and the suffix separately.

Suffixes *-ly*, *-ful*, *-er*, *-or*

Spelling Words

| cheerful | visitor | slowly | weekly | teacher | helper |
| hardly | graceful | yearly | quickly | fighter | sailor |

Use the base word and the new suffix to write a list word.

1. Change **slower** to a word that ends with **-ly**.

   1. _____

2. Change **helpful** to a word that ends with **-er**.

   2. _____

3. Change **quickest** to a word that ends with **-ly**.

   3. _____

4. Change **harder** to a word that ends with **-ly**.

   4. _____

5. Change **sailing** to a word that ends in **-or**.

   5. _____

6. Change **teaching** to a word that ends in **-er**.

   6. _____

Write the list words in the box in ABC order.

| graceful |
| visitor |
| cheerful |
| yearly |
| fighter |
| weekly |

7. _____   8. _____

9. _____   10. _____

11. _____   12. _____

School + Home

Home Activity: Your child has been learning to spell words with the suffixes *-ly*, *-ful*, *-er*, and *-or*. Look through printed material to find other words with these suffixes.

Name _____

Prefixes *un-*, *re-*, *pre-*, *dis-*

Generalization When prefixes **un-**, **re-**, **pre-**, and **dis-** are added to most words, the base word stays the same.

Sort the list words by their prefixes.

un-

1. _____

2. _____

3. _____

4. _____

re-

5. _____

6. _____

7. _____

8. _____

pre-

9. _____

10. _____

dis-

11. _____

12. _____

Challenge Words

un-

13. _____

pre-

14. _____

re-

15. _____

Copyright © Savvas Learning Company LLC. All Rights Reserved.

Spelling Words
1. unsafe
2. preheat
3. rerun
4. disappear
5. unlock
6. retie
7. rewind
8. unpack
9. unplug
10. regroup
11. preschool
12. disagree
Challenge Words
13. prehistoric
14. unfortunate
15. reunion

Home Activity Your child is learning to spell words with the prefixes *un-*, *re-*, *pre-*, and *dis-*. To practice at home, have your child look at the word, say it, spell it, and identify the base word.

Prefixes *un-*, *re-*, *pre-*, *dis-*

Write the list word.

Spelling Words	
unsafe	rewind
preheat	unpack
rerun	unplug
disappear	regroup
unlock	preschool
retie	disagree

not safe

wind again

1. _____

2. _____

opposite of pack

group in a new way

3. _____

4. _____

Read the sentence. Make a list word by adding a prefix to the underlined word.

5. Did you <u>plug</u> the lamp?

_____

6. I <u>agree</u> with that idea.

_____

7. Let's <u>run</u> those home movies.

_____

8. Eddie started <u>school</u> this year.

_____

9. Be sure to <u>lock</u> the door.

_____

10. My cat seems to <u>appear</u> at night.

_____

11. Please <u>tie</u> your shoes.

_____

12. Did you <u>heat</u> the oven?

_____

Home Activity Your child spelled words with the prefixes *un-*, *re-*, *pre-*, and *dis-*. Have your child explain how the new word changes the meaning of the sentences in Exercises 5 to 12 above.

Prefixes *un-*, *re-*, *pre-*, *dis-*

Read Denny's note. **Circle** three spelling mistakes. **Write** the words correctly. **Write** the word that needs a capital letter.

Hey, I found out where your dogs go when they disapear. I saw them when I was riding my bike. they were playing with the boys at the preskool. I sed I'd find out, and I did!

Denny

Spelling Words

unsafe	rewind
preheat	unpack
rerun	unplug
disappear	regroup
unlock	preschool
retie	disagree

1. _____

2. _____

3. _____

4. _____

Frequently Misspelled Words

upon

said

was

Circle the word that is spelled correctly. **Write** it.

5. unpack   inpack   5. _____

6. perheet   preheat   6. _____

7. disagre   disagree   7. _____

8. regroup   rigroup   8. _____

9. unsav   unsafe   9. _____

10. rewind   rewine   10. _____

Home Activity Your child identified misspelled words with the prefixes *un-*, *re-*, *pre-*, and *dis-*. Pronounce a list word. Ask your child to identify the prefix and spell the word.

Spelling Practice Book

Prefixes *un-*, *re-*, *pre-*, *dis-*

Spelling Words					
unsafe	rerun	unlock	rewind	unplug	preschool
preheat	disappear	retie	unpack	regroup	disagree

Write the list word that matches each clue.

1. This word rhymes with **kind** but starts with **w**. Add the prefix **re-**.

2. This word rhymes with **treat** but starts with **h**. Add the prefix **pre-**.

3. This word rhymes with **pie**, but starts with **t**. Add the prefix **re-**.

4. This word rhymes with **bug**, but starts with **pl**. Add the prefix **un-**.

1. _____

2. _____

3. _____

4. _____

Draw a line to match the prefix to the base. **Write** the word.

pre   run   5. _____

un   school   6. _____

re   agree   7. _____

dis   safe   8. _____

Home Activity Your child has been learning to spell words with the prefixes *un-*, *re-*, *pre-*, and *dis-*. Help your child search through a magazine or other printed material for other words with these prefixes.

Words with *kn, wr, gn, mb*

Generalization Sometimes two letters together stand for only one sound: <u>kn</u>ee, <u>wr</u>ite, si<u>gn</u>, and co<u>mb</u>.

Sort the list words by **kn**, **wr**, **gn**, and **mb**.

kn
_____
1. _____
2. _____
3. _____

mb
4. _____
5. _____
6. _____

gn
_____
7. _____
8. _____

wr
9. _____
10. _____
11. _____
12. _____

Challenge Words

kn
13. _____

mb
14. _____

wr
15. _____

Spelling Words
1. knock
2. sign
3. knee
4. wrong
5. write
6. climb
7. wrap
8. wren
9. gnat
10. lamb
11. comb
12. knob

Challenge Words
13. knuckle
14. wrestle
15. plumber

Home Activity Your child is learning to spell words with *kn*, *wr*, *gn*, and *mb*. To practice at home, have your child write the word, say it and then circle the letters that stand together but have one sound.

Words with *kn*, *wr*, *gn*, *mb*

Write list words to name the pictures.

Spelling Words	
knock	wrap
sign	wren
knee	gnat
wrong	lamb
write	comb
climb	knob

1. _____

2. _____

Keep off the Grass

3. _____

4. _____

Write the list word that means almost the same as each word or phrase.

5. tap _____

6. young sheep _____

7. print _____

8. little fly _____

9. incorrect _____

10. go up _____

11. small bird _____

12. cover with paper _____

School + Home

Home Activity Your child spelled words with *kn*, *wr*, *gn*, and *mb*. Have your child point out examples of these letter combinations.

Spelling Practice Book

Name _____

Words with *kn, wr, gn, mb*

Read Jessie's report. **Circle** three spelling mistakes. **Write** the words correctly. **Cross out** the wrong verb in the second sentence. **Write** the correct verb.

> I saw some people clim up a rock wall. One person done something rong. He hurt his knee. I woud like to try rock climbing.

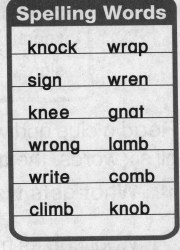

Spelling Words	
knock	wrap
sign	wren
knee	gnat
wrong	lamb
write	comb
climb	knob

1. _____

2. _____

3. _____

4. _____

Frequently Misspelled Words

Christmas

knew

would

what

Fill in the circle next to the word that is spelled correctly.

5. ○ knok   ○ knock   ○ nock   ○ knoke

6. ○ wrin   ○ ren   ○ wren   ○ rwen

7. ○ sign   ○ sine   ○ signe   ○ sien

8. ○ com   ○ komb   ○ kome   ○ comb

9. ○ lam   ○ lamm   ○ lamb   ○ labm

10. ○ writ   ○ write   ○ rite   ○ wriet

School + Home

Home Activity Your child identified misspelled words with *kn, wr, gn,* and *mb*. Pronounce a list word. Ask your child to spell the word and name the "silent letter." (*k, w, g,* or *b*)

Bad Dog, Dodger!
REVIEW

Words with *kn*, *wr*, *gn*, *mb*

Spelling Words

knock	knee	write	wrap	gnat	comb
sign	wrong	climb	wren	lamb	knob

Read a clue and write the list word. When you have written all six words, the answer to the riddle will appear in the boxes.

What gets wetter and wetter the more it dries?

1. Wool comes from this animal. ___ ⬜ ___ ___

2. You do this with a pencil. ___ ___ ___ ⬜ ___

3. You pull this to open a cabinet. ___ ___ ⬜ ___

4. You do this to a gift. ⬜ ___ ___ ___

5. This is part of your leg. ___ ___ ⬜ ___

6. You do this to get up in a tree. ___ ___ ⬜ ___ ___

Write the list words in the box in ABC order.

7. _____   8. _____

9. _____   10. _____

11. _____   12. _____

knock	gnat
sign	wren
wrong	comb

Home Activity Your child has been learning to spell words with *kn*, *wr*, *gn*, and *mb*. Have your child create and write a sentence using two or more of the list words.

Consonant Sound /f/

Generalization The consonant sound /f/ can be spelled **ph**, **gh**, **ff**, and **ffe**: p**h**one, enou**gh**, stu**ff**, and gira**ffe**.

Sort the list words by **ph**, **gh**, **ff**, and **ffe**.

ph

1. _____

2. _____

3. _____

ff

4. _____

5. _____

6. _____

gh

7. _____

8. _____

9. _____

10. _____

11. _____

ffe

12. _____

Challenge Words

ph

13. _____

14. _____

15. _____

Spelling Words
1. phone
2. enough
3. stuff
4. laugh
5. puff
6. giraffe
7. graph
8. tough
9. photo
10. rough
11. cough
12. cliff

Challenge Words

13. dolphin

14. physical

15. autograph

Home Activity Your child is learning words with the sound of *f* spelled *ph*, *gh*, *ff*, and *ffe*. To practice at home, ask you child to write each list word on a piece of paper. Then ask your child to identify the consonants that make the sound of *f*.

Consonant Sound /f/

Write a list word to answer the riddles.

What rhymes with **bone** and starts with **ph**?
_____

1. _____

What rhymes with **cuff** and starts with **p**?
_____

2. _____

What rhymes with **bluff** and starts with **st**?
_____

3. _____

What rhymes with **stiff** and starts with **cl**?
_____

4. _____

Spelling Words	
phone	graph
enough	tough
stuff	photo
laugh	rough
puff	cough
giraffe	cliff

Write the list word that means almost the same as each word or phrase.

5. plenty _____

6. chart _____

7. not smooth _____

8. snapshot _____

Write the list word that best fits in each sentence.

9. What questions do you have about a _____ ?

10. This steak is _____ .

11. The joke made me _____ .

12. He took medicine for his _____ .

School + Home **Home Activity** Your child wrote words with the sound of *f* spelled *ph*, *gh*, *ff*, and *ffe*. Take turns with your child pointing to and spelling the list words.

Consonant Sound /f/

Read the poem. **Circle** three spelling mistakes. **Write** the words correctly. Find a line with a missing end mark. Add the end mark.

Spelling Words	
phone	graph
enough	tough
stuff	photo
laugh	rough
puff	cough
giraffe	cliff

I wrote this poem about the cold
I caught from my frend.

    A Cold

It hurts to laugh.
My throat feels ruf.
I have to cough
I've had enouff!

Frequently Misspelled Words

different

friend

I. _____

2. _____

3. _____

Circle the word that is spelled correctly.

4. The _____ is ringing. ◯ fone ◯ phone

5. I put your _____ in a box. ◯ stuf ◯ stuff

6. That _____ of wind felt good. ◯ puff ◯ puf

7. The _____ is eating leaves. ◯ girafe ◯ giraffe

8. Did you get _____ to eat? ◯ enough ◯ enouf

9. The joke made me _____. ◯ lauff ◯ laugh

10. I need some _____ paper. ◯ graph ◯ gragh

Home Activity Your child has been learning words with the sound of *f* spelled *ph*, *gh*, *ff*, and *ffe*. Ask your child to find examples of these letter combinations in the list words.

Name _____

Consonant Sound /f/

Spelling Words					
phone	enough	stuff	laugh	puff	giraffe
graph	tough	photo	rough	cough	cliff

Circle these words in the puzzle. **Search** across, down, and diagonally.

1. enough
2. cliff
3. tough
4. giraffe
5. puff
6. cough
7. stuff

```
s  g  i  r  a  f  f  e  p
c  o  s  t  u  g  h  c  u
t  l  e  n  t  o  u  g  h
c  n  i  g  h  p  i  t  o
o  o  p  f  i  n  u  p  f
u  u  c  l  f  p  e  f  c
g  e  n  o  u  g  h  e  f
h  s  c  i  z  o  u  g  h
t  f  l  s  t  u  f  f  h
```

Replace F with the correct letters. **Write** the list word.

8. lauF _____

9. Fone _____

10. graF _____

11. rouF _____

12. Foto _____

School + Home

Home Activity Your child has been learning words with the sound of *f* spelled *ph*, *gh*, *ff*, and *ffe*. Write a list word, omitting these letter combinations. Ask your child to complete the word.

Spelling Practice Book

Vowel Sound in *fall*

Generalization The vowel sound in *fall* can be spelled **aw**, **au**, **augh**, and **al**: dr**aw**, **au**to, c**augh**t, and t**al**k.

Sort the words by **aw**, **au**, **augh**, and **al**.

aw

1. _____

2. _____

au

3. _____

4. _____

5. _____

6. _____

7. _____

augh

8. _____

9. _____

al

10. _____

11. _____

12. _____

Challenge Words

aw

13. _____

au

14. _____

15. _____

Spelling Words
1. talk
2. because
3. August
4. caught
5. draw
6. walk
7. chalk
8. auto
9. taught
10. thaw
11. fault
12. launch
Challenge Words
13. applause
14. audience
15. awkward

Home Activity Your child is learning words with the vowel sound in *fall* spelled *aw*, *au*, *augh*, and *al*. To practice at home, have your child say the word, study the spelling of the vowel sound, and then write the word.

The Signmaker's Assistant
PRACTICE

Vowel Sound in *fall*

Spelling Words					
talk	because	August	caught	draw	walk
chalk	auto	taught	thaw	fault	launch

Read the word. **Write** a related list word.

1. blackboard: _____

2. mouth: _____

3. teach: _____

4. road: _____

5. month: _____

6. artist: _____

7. path: _____

8. warm: _____

Write the missing list words.

9. Let's _____ the boat!

10. It was his _____ that we missed the bus.

11. I am happy _____ I won the game.

12. She _____ three fish.

Home Activity Your child wrote words with the vowel sound in *fall* spelled *aw*, *au*, *augh*, and *al*. Ask your child how all the list words are the same. (All have the vowel sound found in *fall*; all have an *a* in combination with other letters.)

Spelling Practice Book

Vowel Sound in *fall*

Read the letter. **Circle** three spelling mistakes and a word that needs a capital letter. **Write** the words correctly.

Spelling Words	
talk	chalk
because	auto
August	taught
caught	thaw
draw	fault
walk	launch

August 5

Dear aunt Helen,
    Thank you for the big box of chauk. I used it to drawer pictures all over the walk. Everyone thot they were beautiful!

Love,
Janie

Frequently Misspelled Words

thought

caught

1. _____

2. _____

3. _____

4. _____

Circle the misspelled list word. **Write** each word correctly.

5. The ice will thau.

5. _____

6. Who talt you how to swim?

6. _____

7. I left becus I felt sick.

7. _____

8. He runs an aughto repair shop.

8. _____

School + Home

Home Activity Your child identified misspelled words with the vowel sound in *fall* spelled *aw*, *au*, *augh*, and *al*. Give clues about a spelling word. Ask your child to guess and spell it.

Name _____

Vowel Sound in *fall*

Spelling Words					
talk	because	August	caught	draw	walk
chalk	auto	taught	thaw	fault	launch

Finish the list words in the box. Each word has been started.

1. l	2. b	3. A
4. d	5. th	6. w
7. f	8. a	9. ch

Unscramble the list word. **Write** it.

10. augh t t _____

11. t augh c _____

12. k t al _____

Home Activity Your child has been learning words with the vowel sound in *fall* spelled *aw, au, augh,* and *al*. Toss a coin onto the box above and read the word. Can your child correctly spell the word without looking? Take turns tossing the coin and spelling words.

Spelling Practice Book

Contractions

Generalization In contractions, an apostrophe (') takes the place of letters that are left out: **we are** becomes **we're**.

Sort the list words by the type of contraction.

are
_____
1. _____
2. _____
3. _____

have
_____
4. _____
5. _____

not
_____
6. _____
7. _____
8. _____

had/would
_____
9. _____
10. _____
11. _____
12. _____

Challenge Words

have
_____
13. _____
14. _____
15. _____

Spelling Words
1. we're
2. I've
3. don't
4. can't
5. he'd
6. you're
7. won't
8. they're
9. I'd
10. they'd
11. she'd
12. we've
Challenge Words
13. could've
14. would've
15. should've

Home Activity Your child is learning to spell contractions. To practice at home, ask you child to read each word. Help your child make a sentence using each list word. Then make the same sentence using the two words used to make the contraction.

Contractions

Spelling Words					
we're	I've	don't	can't	he'd	you're
won't	they're	I'd	they'd	she'd	we've

Combine the two words into a contraction.

1. we + are _____

2. they + had _____

3. do + not _____

4. she + would _____

5. they + are _____

6. you + are _____

7. we + have _____

8. will + not _____

Write a contraction that could be used instead of the underlined words.

9. <u>I have</u> been riding the roller coaster. _____

10. We <u>cannot</u> go on the bumper cars. _____

11. I know <u>I would</u> like some popcorn. _____

12. Before today, <u>he had</u> never won a prize. _____

Home Activity Your child spelled words with contractions. Point to a spelling word. Ask your child to name the words that were combined to make the contraction.

Spelling Practice Book

Contractions

Spelling Words					
we're	I've	don't	can't	he'd	you're
won't	they're	I'd	they'd	she'd	we've

Read the directions. **Circle** three spelling mistakes. **Write** the words correctly. **Cross out** the extra word in the first sentence.

Frequently Misspelled Words
don't
they're
there's

Go to the the cave. There's a bear inside.
It wo'nt hurt you.

Walk northeast until your at the river. Remember, dont cross into the woods!

Dig under the big rock.

Good luck!

1. _____

2. _____

3. _____

Fill in the circle next to the word that is spelled correctly.

4. ○ she'd   ○ sheed   ○ shee'd

5. ○ the'yre   ○ theyr'e   ○ they're

6. ○ cann't   ○ can't   ○ can'nt

7. ○ wer'e   ○ wu're   ○ we're

8. ○ Ive   ○ I've   ○ Iv'e

Home Activity Your child has been learning to spell words with contractions. Your child may enjoy creating a treasure map. Use colored pencils on crumpled paper. Include some contractions in the map directions.

Spelling Practice Book

Unit 6 Week 1 **Day 3** **103**

Contractions

Spelling Words					
we're	I've	don't	can't	he'd	you're
won't	they're	I'd	they'd	she'd	we've

Cross out all of these letters: **j, p, m, b. Write** a list word by copying the letters that are left.

j m w p e ' v m e

1. _____

p j m p I ' d p j

2. _____

b h j p e ' m d b

3. _____

y b o j u ' r b e

4. _____

j b t h m e j y ' d

5. _____

b d m o p n ' t b

6. _____

b w m e ' r p e b

7. _____

b I b ' v e m j

8. _____

t p h e m y ' r b e

9. _____

Write the missing list word. It will rhyme with the underlined word.

10. <u>We'd</u> like to sit in the sun, but _____ rather run.

11. If you <u>don't</u> want to run very far, we _____ .

12. The dog _____ run any longer. She can only <u>pant</u>.

Home Activity Your child has been learning to spell words with contractions. Remind your child that the apostrophe (') in the contraction should always be placed in the spot where the letters are missing.

Name _____

More Adding -*ed* and -*ing*

Generalization The spelling of the base word is often changed when adding
-ed but kept when adding -ing: tr<u>ied</u>, tr<u>ying</u>.

Sort the list words by -**ed** or -**ing**.

-ed	-ing
1. _____	7. _____
2. _____	8. _____
3. _____	9. _____
4. _____	10. _____
5. _____	11. _____
6. _____	12. _____

Spelling Words
1. tried
2. trying
3. planned
4. planning
5. liked
6. liking
7. hiked
8. hiking
9. cried
10. crying
11. skipped
12. skipping
Challenge Words
13. danced
14. dancing
15. replied
16. replying

Challenge Words

-ed	-ing
13. _____	15. _____
14. _____	16. _____

Home Activity Your child is learning to spell words that end with -*ed* or -*ing*. To practice at home, have your child say the word, study the word ending, and then spell the word aloud.

More Adding *-ed* and *-ing*

Spelling Words					
tried	trying	planned	planning	liked	liking
hiked	hiking	cried	crying	skipped	skipping

Write the missing list word. It rhymes with the underlined word.

1. They <u>biked</u> and _____ in the park.

2. We would have _____ to have <u>biked</u> this afternoon.

3. Chris _____ when her fish <u>died</u>.

4. I kept <u>tripping</u> as I was _____ rope.

5. Have you _____ this <u>fried</u> chicken?

6. Mom is _____ on <u>canning</u> some tomatoes.

Find two list words that follow each rule. **Write** the words.

Drop the final **e** before adding **-ing** to the base word.	Double the final consonant before adding **-ed** to the base word.	Just add **-ing** to the base word.
7. _____	9. _____	11. _____
8. _____	10. _____	12. _____

Home Activity Your child spelled words that end with *-ed* and *-ing*. Point to a spelling word. Have your child pronounce and spell the base word and tell whether the base word changed when the ending was added.

Spelling Practice Book

More Adding *-ed* and *-ing*

Read the word puzzle. **Circle** two words that are spelled wrong and a word that is missing its *-ing* ending. **Write** the words correctly.

Spelling Words	
tried	hiked
trying	hiking
planned	cried
planning	crying
liked	skipped
liking	skipping

Everyone tryed to be first in line.

A girl who skiped rope was first. She is smiling.

A girl who liked wearing bows in her hair is behind a girl who is cry.

Who is last in line?

(Answer: The girl wearing bows in her hair)

Frequently Misspelled Words

thought

caught

1. _____

2. _____

3. _____

Circle the word that is spelled correctly.

4.	planing	planning	plainning
5.	cryed	cryied	cried
6.	skipping	skiping	skipng
7.	liked	likeed	likd
8.	planed	planned	pland
9.	hikking	hikeing	hiking
10.	tring	trying	tryeing

Home Activity Pronounce a base word. Ask your child to spell the corresponding *-ed* and *-ing* words.

More Adding -ed and -ing

Spelling Words

tried	trying	planned	planning	liked	liking
hiked	hiking	cried	crying	skipped	skipping

Unscramble the letters to make a list word.

1. k l d e i
_____
- - - - - - - - - - - - -

2. i c n r y g
_____
- - - - - - - - - - - - -

3. e p s i p k d
_____
- - - - - - - - - - - - -

4. k n i i l g
_____
- - - - - - - - - - - - -

5. e t d r i
_____
- - - - - - - - - - - - -

6. n i k i h g
_____
- - - - - - - - - - - - -

Write the missing words. Then use the numbered letters
to write the missing word in the sentence.

7. He is ____ to learn chess.
___ ___ ___ ___ ___
    2   4

8. I ____ my report.
___ ___ ___ ___ ___
                6

9. He ____ when he got hurt.
___ ___ ___ ___
    3

10. She is good at ____ rope.
___ ___ ___ ___ ___
1   5

If he makes one more ___ ___ ___ ___ ___ ___**, he is out.**
1   2   3   4   5   6

Home Activity Your child has been spelling words that end with -ed and -ing. Have your child
identify and spell the four words that are most difficult for him or her.

Words with -*tion* and -*ture*

Generalization The final syllables in *mixture* and *nation* have the common syllable patterns **-ture** and **-tion**.

Sort the list words by **-ture** or **-tion**.

-ture

_____

1. _____

2. _____

3. _____

4. _____

5. _____

6. _____

-tion

_____

7. _____

8. _____

9. _____

10. _____

11. _____

12. _____

Spelling Words
1. mixture
2. nation
3. section
4. future
5. picture
6. action
7. caution
8. station
9. fixture
10. motion
11. nature
12. feature

Challenge Words

13. furniture
14. adventure
15. tuition

Challenge Words

-ture

_____

13. _____

14. _____

-tion

_____

15. _____

Home Activity Your child is learning to spell words with -*tion* and -*ture*. To practice at home, have your child look at the word, say it, spell it, and then write it on a piece of paper. Ask your child to point to the common syllable pattern.

Words with *-tion* and *-ture*

Spelling Words					
mixture	nation	section	future	picture	action
caution	station	fixture	motion	nature	feature

Write a list word.

It rhymes with **fraction**, but it starts like **apple**.

1. _____

It rhymes with **notion**, but it starts like **mop**.

2. _____

It rhymes with **mixture**, but it starts like **fan**.

3. _____

It rhymes with **station**, but it starts like **nap**.

4. _____

It rhymes with **creature**, but it starts like **fix**.

5. _____

It rhymes with **fixture**, but it starts like **mat**.

6. _____

Write the missing list word.

7. Proceed with _____.

8. It's time for a _____ break.

9. We went on a _____ walk.

10. I get the _____ .

11. Where's the sports _____ of the paper?

12. It's a job with a _____ .

Home Activity Your child spelled words with *-tion* and *-ture*. Have your child circle *-tion* or *-ture* in each word.

Spelling Practice Book

Words with *-tion* and *-ture*

Spelling Words					
mixture	nation	section	future	picture	action
caution	station	fixture	motion	nature	feature

Read the poster. **Circle** three spelling words and one word with a capitalization error. **Write** the words correctly.

_____

1. _____

2. _____

3. _____

4. _____

Special double featur!

Packed with ACTION

A superhero of the future saves the naton.

Bring the famly saturday at 1:00.

Frequently Misspelled Words

special

family

really

Circle the word that is spelled correctly. **Write** it.

_____

5. caution   causion   _____

6. nater   nature   _____

7. picture   pichure   _____

8. section   sectshion   _____

Home Activity Your child identified misspelled words with *–tion* and *–ture*. Have your child underline these letter combinations in the list words.

Words with *-tion* and *-ture*

Spelling Words					
mixture	nation	section	future	picture	action
caution	station	fixture	motion	nature	feature

Crossword Puzzle

Write list words in the puzzle.

Across
3. care
4. a country
5. a part

Down
1. a drawing
2. movement

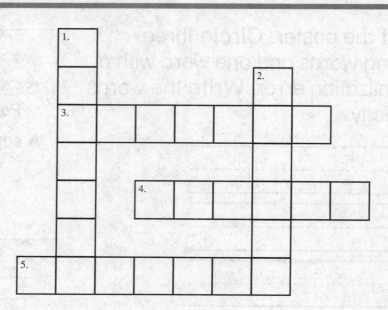

Circle the word that comes first in a dictionary. **Write** it.

6. caution   action   feature   _____

7. section   station   mixture   _____

8. picture   future   nation   _____

9. nature   picture   section   _____

10. mixture   nature   fixture   _____

Home Activity Your child has been learning to spell words with *-tion* and *-ture*. Point to a spelling word. Have your child spell the word and use it in a sentence.

Spelling Practice Book

Suffixes *-ness* and *-less*

Generalization When **-ness** or **-less** is added to most base words, the base word stays the same: **kind<u>ness</u>, care<u>less</u>**.

Sort the list words by **-ness** and **-less**.

-ness

1. _____
2. _____
3. _____
4. _____
5. _____
6. _____
7. _____

-less

8. _____
9. _____
10. _____
11. _____
12. _____

Challenge Words

-ness

13. _____
14. _____

-less

15. _____

Spelling Words

1. kindness
2. careless
3. goodness
4. useless
5. fearless
6. darkness
7. sadness
8. sickness
9. helpless
10. thankless
11. fitness
12. weakness

Challenge Words

13. awareness
14. eagerness
15. wireless

School + Home

Home Activity Your child is learning to spell words with *-ness* and *-less*. To practice at home, have your child write the list word and circle the base word. Ask if the base word stayed the same.

Spelling Practice Book

Suffixes *-ness* and *-less*

Spelling Words					
kindness	careless	goodness	useless	fearless	darkness
sadness	sickness	helpless	thankless	fitness	weakness

Write a list word that means the same as each word or phrase.

sorrow

1. _____

being fit

2. _____

being good

3. _____

without help

4. _____

being kind

5. _____

not rewarded

6. _____

Write a list word to finish each sentence.

7. Grandma has a _____ for sweets.

8. His _____ caused a high fever.

9. I stumbled in the _____ .

10. It's _____ to look for his ring in the lake.

11. The _____ firefighters rescued the little boy.

12. I was _____ and dropped my model airplane.

Home Activity Your child used spelling words in sentences. Have your child make up new sentences, using the list words.

Spelling Practice Book

Name _____

Suffixes -ness and -less

Spelling Words					
kindness	careless	goodness	useless	fearless	darkness
sadness	sickness	helpless	thankless	fitness	weakness

Read the story. **Circle** three spelling mistakes. **Write** the words correctly. **Write** the run-on sentence as two separate sentences.

Last night I heard a scratchy noise in the darknes. My fearless sister got up she turned on the light. My hamster was scratching under my bed. I hadn't put him back in his cage. I won't be so carless agin!

Frequently Misspelled Words

again

very

then

1. _____   2. _____   3. _____

4. _____

Circle the word that is spelled correctly. **Write** it.

5. sickness   _____
   sicknes

6. usless   _____
   useless

7. weakness   _____
   weekness

8. sadness   _____
   sadnes

School + Home

Home Activity Your child identified misspelled words with -ness and -less. Have your child pronounce a list word and then spell the base word and the suffix separately.

Name _____

Suffixes -*ness* and -*less*

Spelling Words

kindness	careless	goodness	useless	fearless	darkness
sadness	sickness	helpless	thankless	fitness	weakness

Finish the list words. **Read** the word in the shaded boxes to find something that grows on reefs.

weakness
careless
sickness
helpless
goodness

I.		i				e	s	s
2.				d		e	s	s
3.		a				e	s	s
4.	w					e	s	s
5.				p		e	s	s

Fill the chart with list words.

	Base Word	-ness	-less
6.	sad		
7.	use		
8.	dark		
9.	thank		
10.	fit		
11.	fear		
12.	kind		

Home Activity Your child has been learning to spell words with -*ness* and -*less*. Help your child look in schoolbooks or library books for examples of words with these suffixes.

Spelling Practice Book

Prefixes *mis-* and *mid-*

Generalization When **mis-** and **mid-** are added to words, make no change in the spelling of the base word: **mid** + **air** = **midair**.

Sort the list words by **mis-** and **mid-**.

mis-

1. _____

2. _____

3. _____

4. _____

5. _____

6. _____

7. _____

mid-

8. _____

9. _____

10. _____

11. _____

12. _____

Challenge Words

mis-

13. _____

mid-

14. _____

15. _____

Spelling Words

1. midair
2. misplace
3. mislead
4. midway
5. misprint
6. midday
7. midweek
8. misbehave
9. midyear
10. mismatch
11. misdeed
12. mistake

Challenge Words

13. midstream
14. midnight
15. misbehavior

Home Activity Your child is learning to spell words with the prefixes *mis-* and *mid-*. To practice at home, ask your child to identify the prefixes for each word. Then ask your child to spell each list word.

Prefixes *mis-* and *mid-*

Spelling Words					
midair	misplace	mislead	midway	misprint	midday
midweek	misbehave	midyear	mismatch	misdeed	mistake

Write a list word by adding mid- or mis to each base word.

match

1. _____

print

2. _____

week

3. _____

air

4. _____

behave

5. _____

deed

6. _____

year

7. _____

way

8. _____

Write the missing list word to complete each phrase.

_____

9. _____ your keys

10. make a _____

11. _____ people

12. _____ nap

School + Home

Home Activity Your child wrote spelling words in sentences. Take turns with your child using the words in new sentences.

Name _____

Prefixes *mis-* and *mid-*

Read the notice. **Circle** three spelling mistakes and a word with a capitalization error. **Write** the words correctly.

Notice: There was a missprint in last week's newsletter. The class book fair will **not** be misweek. It will be after school on friday. We are sorry about the mistake. We didn't mean to mislead you. We hope evry student can come!

Spelling Words	
midair	misplace
mislead	midway
misprint	midday
midweek	misbehave
midyear	mismatch
misdeed	mistake

1. _____

2. _____

3. _____

4. _____

Frequently Misspelled Words

every

whole

could

Circle the word that is spelled correctly. **Write** the word.

5. midway   middway   5. _____

6. misbehav   misbehave   6. _____

7. mislead   misleed   7. _____

8. misplace   misplase   8. _____

Home Activity Your child identified misspelled words with *mis-* and *mid-*. Pronounce a list word. Have your child spell the base word and the prefix separately.

Prefixes *mis-* and *mid-*

Spelling Words

midair	misplace	mislead	midway	misprint	midday
midweek	misbehave	midyear	mismatch	misdeed	mistake

Unscramble each word.

k i m d e e w

----

1. _____

h a b v e s i m e

----

3. _____

e e s i d d m

----

5. _____

d e a l m i s

----

2. _____

r a m i i d

----

4. _____

s t a m i k e

----

6. _____

Write the list word.

7. This word rhymes with **trace**, but starts with **pl**. Add the prefix **mis-**.

8. This word rhymes with **clear**, but starts with **y**. Add the prefix **mid-**.

9. This word rhymes with **scratch**, but starts with **m**. Add the prefix **mis-**.

10. This word rhymes with **stay**, but starts with **w**. Add the prefix **mid-**.

7. _____

----

8. _____

----

9. _____

----

10. _____

Home Activity Your child has been learning to spell words with *mis-* and *mid-*. Take turns with your child thinking of a base word and adding *mis-* or *mid-* to make a list word.

Digraphs *ch, tch, sh, th, wh*

Unit 1, Week 5

1. bunch
2. that
3. wish
4. patch
5. when
6. what
7. math
8. them
9. shape
10. whale
11. itch
12. chase

Adding *-ed* and *-ing*

Unit 1, Week 4

1. talked
2. talking
3. dropped
4. dropping
5. excited
6. exciting
7. lifted
8. lifting
9. hugged
10. hugging
11. smiled
12. smiling

Consonant Blends

Unit 1, Week 3

1. stop
2. strap
3. nest
4. hand
5. brave
6. ask
7. clip
8. stream
9. mask
10. twin
11. breeze
12. state

Long Vowels CVCe

Unit 1, Week 2

1. tune
2. page
3. nose
4. space
5. size
6. fine
7. mice
8. late
9. cube
10. blaze
11. home
12. vote

Short Vowels CVC, CVCC, CCVC

Unit 1, Week 1

1. drum
2. rock
3. list
4. desk
5. job
6. sad
7. chop
8. sack
9. tag
10. rib
11. mess
12. dust

Long *a*: *ai*, *ay*

Unit 2, Week 5

1. tail
2. main
3. wait
4. say
5. away
6. play

7. raise
8. brain
9. paint
10. stay
11. today
12. tray

Adding -*s*, -*es*

Unit 2, Week 4

1. note
2. notes
3. lunch
4. lunches
5. story
6. stories

7. tune
8. tunes
9. switch
10. switches
11. baby
12. babies

Words with *er*, *ir*, *ur*

Unit 2, Week 3

1. her
2. person
3. nurse
4. dirt
5. turn
6. birth

7. serve
8. curb
9. curl
10. skirt
11. purse
12. turtle

Contractions

Unit 2, Week 2

1. I'll
2. wasn't
3. it's
4. he's
5. I'm
6. didn't

7. who's
8. she's
9. we'll
10. isn't
11. hasn't
12. hadn't

Words with *ar*, *or*, *ore*

Unit 2, Week 1

1. part
2. hard
3. born
4. horse
5. before
6. more

7. smart
8. farm
9. porch
10. corn
11. chore
12. score

Adding -er and -est

Unit 3, Week 5

1. sooner
2. soonest
3. hotter
4. hottest
5. busier
6. busiest
7. happier
8. happiest
9. smaller
10. smallest
11. fatter
12. fattest

Long i: i, igh, y

Unit 3, Week 4

1. find
2. child
3. sky
4. bright
5. wild
6. fly
7. right
8. flight
9. spider
10. cry
11. blind
12. myself

Compound Words

Unit 3, Week 3

1. basketball
2. someone
3. weekend
4. something
5. birthday
6. riverbank
7. bathtub
8. backyard
9. driveway
10. bedtime
11. raindrop
12. mailbox

Long o: o, oa, ow

Unit 3, Week 2

1. goat
2. hold
3. show
4. most
5. bowl
6. float
7. toast
8. ago
9. open
10. told
11. toad
12. slow

Long e: ee, ea, y

Unit 3, Week 1

1. read
2. feel
3. easy
4. deep
5. seat
6. party
7. wheel
8. leave
9. windy
10. sleep
11. teeth
12. team

Vowel Sound in *moon*

Unit 4, Week 5

1. too
2. new
3. fruit
4. blue
5. true
6. cool
7. suit
8. spoon
9. clue
10. juice
11. drew
12. flew

Vowel Sound in *joy*

Unit 4, Week 4

1. joy
2. noise
3. royal
4. moist
5. broil
6. cowboy
7. spoil
8. joint
9. foil
10. enjoy
11. destroy
12. loyal

Vowel Sound in *gown*

Unit 4, Week 3

1. around
2. about
3. gown
4. sound
5. flower
6. howl
7. ground
8. pound
9. crown
10. south
11. mouse
12. downtown

Vowel Sound in *book*

Unit 4, Week 2

1. put
2. cook
3. stood
4. full
5. wood
6. July
7. shook
8. push
9. pull
10. brook
11. hook
12. hood

Words Ending in *-le*

Unit 4, Week 1

1. ankle
2. title
3. apple
4. cable
5. purple
6. able
7. bugle
8. bundle
9. bubble
10. giggle
11. sparkle
12. tickle

Spelling Practice Book

Vowel Sound in *fall*

Unit 5, Week 5

1. talk
2. because
3. August
4. caught
5. draw
6. walk
7. chalk
8. auto
9. taught
10. thaw
11. fault
12. launch

Consonant Sound /f/

Unit 5, Week 4

1. phone
2. enough
3. stuff
4. laugh
5. puff
6. giraffe
7. graph
8. tough
9. photo
10. rough
11. cough
12. cliff

Words with *kn*, *wr*, *gn*, *mb*

Unit 5, Week 3

1. knock
2. sign
3. knee
4. wrong
5. write
6. climb
7. wrap
8. wren
9. gnat
10. lamb
11. comb
12. knob

Prefixes *un-*, *re-*, *pre-*, *dis-*

Unit 5, Week 2

1. unsafe
2. preheat
3. rerun
4. disappear
5. unlock
6. retie
7. rewind
8. unpack
9. unplug
10. regroup
11. preschool
12. disagree

Suffixes *-ly*, *-ful*, *-er*, *-or*

Unit 5, Week 1

1. cheerful
2. visitor
3. slowly
4. weekly
5. teacher
6. helper
7. hardly
8. graceful
9. yearly
10. quickly
11. fighter
12. sailor

Spelling Practice Book

129

Prefixes *mis-* and *mid-*

Unit 6, Week 5

1. midair
2. misplace
3. mislead
4. midway
5. misprint
6. midday
7. midweek
8. misbehave
9. midyear
10. mismatch
11. misdeed
12. mistake

Suffixes *-ness* and *-less*

Unit 6, Week 4

1. kindness
2. careless
3. goodness
4. useless
5. fearless
6. darkness
7. sadness
8. sickness
9. helpless
10. thankless
11. fitness
12. weakness

Words with *-tion* and *-ture*

Unit 6, Week 3

1. mixture
2. nation
3. section
4. future
5. picture
6. action
7. caution
8. station
9. fixture
10. motion
11. nature
12. feature

More Adding *-ed* and *-ing*

Unit 6, Week 2

1. tried
2. trying
3. planned
4. planning
5. liked
6. liking
7. hiked
8. hiking
9. cried
10. crying
11. skipped
12. skipping

Contractions

Unit 6, Week 1

1. we're
2. I've
3. don't
4. can't
5. he'd
6. you're
7. won't
8. they're
9. I'd
10. they'd
11. she'd
12. we've